AMERICANS

AN IMPRESSION

BY

ALEXANDER FRANCIS

THOUGH I strive anew
Shadows to pursue,
Shadows vain
Thou'lt remain
  Within my heart.
      JOHN OXENFORD.

LONDON: ANDREW MELROSE
3 YORK STREET, COVENT GARDEN
1909

PREFACE

THE earlier chapters of this book were written in America, the later ones in England; and all were revised by me in Russia, where I was able to regard the two English-speaking nations with greater detachment than was, perhaps, possible either in the country which is my own or in the country which is my theme, and to compare Democracy, as it is exemplified in England and America, with Autocracy, which finds its most notable modern instance in the Empire of the Tsar.

I have higher appreciation of Russians and Russian institutions than most observers of them seem to entertain—possibly, because they know them less; yet, my sense of the value to a people of a democratic government has been deepened by my visit to America and my return from Russia to England. The criticism of American, and inferentially of English, institutions which the following chapters contain implies, therefore, not depreciation of democracy, but appreciation of the need of a purer form and wider application of it than even the most democratic governments display.

In America, as has seemed to me, there is a drift from democracy to an elective despotism; and that I regard as an ominous sign. The election of Mr. Taft to succeed Mr. Roosevelt as President may, however, unless the opinion that I have formed of him is wide of the mark, be taken as a guarantee that the cure of the evils of the democracy will be sought in more, not less, Democracy. Incidentally, I may say that what I have written upon Socialism in America, I had written before the Presidential election had taken place; but the relative strength of political parties discovered by the polls, does not make necessary any modification of the views which I had ventured to express.

I regret that, being removed from my library and my notes, I am unable to give more than the titles of the books to which I refer in the text.

The several chapters of this book first appeared, as a series of special articles, in the London *Times*; and I have pleasure in making grateful acknowledgment of the courtesy of that journal in allowing me to issue them in their present form. I am also deeply indebted

to many Americans, officials and others, for
having given me access to sources of information, and especially for having been themselves
as an open book for me to read. If I could
hope that *Americans* would be read by them,
or by any one, with a moiety of the interest
with which Americans have been read by me,
it would be with less misgiving that I should
send forth this result of my self-imposed and
most pleasurable task.

CALCUTTA, 1909.

CONTENTS

AMERICANS

— ✦ —

CHAPTER I.

THE NATIONAL TEMPER.

"If you wish success in life make Perseverance your bosom Friend,
Experience your wise Counsellor, Caution your elder Brother, and
Hope your Guardian Genius"—ADDISON.

False traditional Estimate of Americans—The Charge of
Materialism—The Era of Brag—Succeeded by excessive
Self-Disparagement—The Faith of the original Settlers—
The Test of national Experience—The present popular
Mood.

I VISITED Americans rather than America. To appreci- Ameri- cans—
I did, indeed, cross and recross the vast
continent, from the Atlantic to the Pacific
Ocean and back to my starting-point, by routes
that carried me over enormous distances, in
such uninterrupted convenience and comfort
(the promiscuous sleeping-cars notwithstanding) as I have not experienced in any, although
I have been across every, other continent of
the world; and I was not insensible, I trust,

to the imposing scenery through which I
passed.   But traversing America was merely
the necessary means to meeting, that I might
know, Americans, which was my constant aim.
For I would fain estimate the genius of the
people ; and how could that be known otherwise than through knowledge of the people
themselves, not only in their outward actions
but also in their inward spirit, in their dominant
emotions and guiding principles as well as in
their achievements in the material world and
the daily habits of their social life?

—a
lifficult
Task—
Who latest attempts this task has the
greatest difficulties to overcome; for the
problem increases in complexity, and becomes
more difficult of solution, as the forces of the
nation, steadily progressing towards some far-
off divine event, daily grow in energy and'
expand in range, ever differentiating themselves into new forms and advancing in the
rapidity of their interaction.   My poor
apparatus, as I know more surely than any
other, can measure only a few feet, if at all,
beneath the surface of this fathomless ocean
which many have sought to sound ; and I make
no pretence, in this or any other chapter, to do
more than give the record made by that
instrument at such depth as, here and there,
it may have reached.

Americans are pre-eminently accessible, and —because, although easily met— to meet them requires nothing more than easy travel.   Their houses lie open to one another and the road, unenclosed by wall, fence or hedge, as if in token of the neighbourliness and friendliness of themselves; and during the year that I was in their country I lived literally *chez eux*.   Excepting a fortnight spent in hotels, my home was with professors in their residences, with students in their "fraternity" chapter-houses, with *alumni* in their university clubs, with ministers in their parsonages, with social workers in their settlements, and with farmers in their homes; and at the moment of writing this, although under my own flag, I am one of the guests of an American who has an island of the Canadian Muskoka Lakes as his summer home.   The strenuous American at work is a familiar sight, but I have had the advantage of also seeing the relaxed American at play; and no man can be known who has not been seen in his recreations as well as at his tasks.   From coast to coast I have also been in touch with immigrants, of whom I shall have much to say, and who, while in process of transformation by native Americans, are exerting far-reaching reactive influence upon them.

But Americans are more easily met than —They are not easily known. known.   Never having had titles of nobility

or clearly defined class distinctions of any kind,
they have not, although some of them are
striving to acquire, the haughtiness and
exclusiveness with which Englishmen are
generally charged, and which are probably due
in England, as Coleridge suggested, not to
climate or natural temper but to the encroachments of classes deemed "lower" on classes
deemed "higher," by which each class became
nervous and jealous in the general communion.
Yet Americans, like other people, practise
reticence and reserve; and, more than other
people, they are other than they seem to
undiscerning eyes. Without intelligence,
sympathy, insight and breadth of view,
observers of them are as idols, having eyes
but seeing not; and the traditional estimate of
Americans is based upon the impressions of
those who, having merely crushed together
several partially observed facts and kneaded
them into an imperfect generalisation which,
being caught up by a violent prejudice, became
a false theory, have spoken and have been
listened to, as if they were gods, pronouncing
judgment upon a great nation which they
themselves were too small to understand.
Americans, with characteristic good-humour,
express their sense of this weakness of ours in
V the story of one of us who, on his return to

England, reported of the speech of Americans that they say "Where am I at?" when we should say "Where is my 'at?" The rebuke is not undeserved.

I am painfully aware that when I first went to America I was under the influence of this false tradition and that, in consequence, there was, even in me who less than the least of all critics have right to it, that "certain condescension on the part of foreigners" which Lowell has so charmingly described. I went at my own instance, to satisfy a vagabond curiosity and under no promise to write, provoked partly by the contrast between Americans as I had found them in Europe and Americans as books declare them to be in their own land. And in the presence of the people and their achievements, after living intimately with them during twelve consecutive months, drinking in, at all the pores of my mental and moral sensibilities, the signs which no one who has any habit of observing men with open heart as well as open mind could fail to discern, I gained a new estimate of the people whom I "went out for to see." I shall have much adverse criticism to offer upon certain aspects of their municipal, political, commercial, educational, domestic and religious life; but, at least, I shall not mistake the sea-foam for the sea.

As dense as most foreigners' ignorance of Americans is many Americans' ignorance of themselves; and the "certain condescension on the part of foreigners" towards all Americans of which I have heard many complaints, is equalled by the condescension of each group of States towards all other groups in the United States. In the North-Western and Western States I have seen the desert made to blossom as the rose before my eyes as marvellously as I have seen a mango grow from seed to fruit beneath the hand of a Hindu juggler; and the settlers, men of English stock and speech, who in the thick of the greatest and swiftest battle ever fought with Nature in her wildest mood remain good-humoured, hospitable and brave, have spoken to me of the Eastern States as a small world of little men who are doing paltry tasks in mean ways. Previously, in the Eastern States, I had been told that, when I got amongst the farmers of the West, I should find them spending all their energy in planting corn to feed swine for sale, in order that with the proceeds they might buy more land on which to plant more corn to feed more swine, in order to get more money to buy still more land on which to plant still more acres of corn to feed still more herds of swine.

These charges, brought by Americans —of Themselves,— against Americans, are but new forms with limited application of the old charge of materialism which has been long brought against the entire American people by the Old World, and which was not disbelieved by me when I came, in much fear and trembling, to this New World. Now, however, after visiting Americans in all parts of their vast territory, I am prepared to undertake the defence of Americans against themselves, and of America against the world and to prove, when occasion shall offer, that the prevalent opinion that America has a double dose of the original sin of materialism is the result of partial observation and mistaken judgment, and is due, in large measure, to the fallacious theory that a people which has proved itself practical and efficient in handling actualities must needs be devoid of spiritual vision, energy and power. Undeniably, there is incessant and devouring activity in all the States of America, except the Southern which are becoming quickly conformist in this as in other respects. Multitudes of Americans are eager for gold and power and put the last things first and the first things last in their ambition and effort; and the prevalent greed and struggle and noise tend to deafen and deaden their highest self and show that they live at the periphery of their being, not knowing where its axis is. It is also undeniable that, as a people, Americans are not as highly developed in their rational and artistic capabilities as in their practical powers, and that consequently America has not yet made contributions to the arts and sciences and the higher intellectual life of the world commensurate with its importance as a national Power. Mediocrity triumphs. Commonness prevails. Yet this is not the whole truth. Beneath the surface, it is found that uniformity does not really exist. Natural replace artificial differences; and there exists, within the one great community, a vast number of smaller communities, each having its special intellectual and moral characteristics. Further, it has to be said that, at the expense of the exceptional it may be, the average has risen. The mountains have, perhaps, been denuded, but the valleys have certainly been raised. Some force has been at work, raising the whole level of the εἰωθότα νοήματα, the ways of thinking and feeling, in which every citizen grows up. To see things in their beauty is to see them in their truth; and this is the beautiful thing that, in America, I have seen —the deep moral foundations on which alone enduring prosperities rest, in this divinely appointed world. The whole people, more completely perhaps. than any other people, have faith in humanity, passion for justice, and devotion to freedom ; and enthusiasm, faith, generous instincts are neither the root nor the fruit of materialism. And although the secular spirit makes itself so apparent that even by the most superficial observer it is not missed, there is a deeper life which has suffered no permanent evil from the gusts of commercial passion with which its surface is constantly swept.

The boy is father to the man ; and the modern American retains as his deepest traits the high and wholesome ideals of the original Colonial settlers. During the years of national growth, the inevitable changes have not been either so radical or so swift as to obliterate all resemblances in the American Republic, in its essential features, to the simple democracies of English Colonial days. Then, there was a virile intellectual, moral and religious life that kept all other interests in reasonable subordination. New England is able, and never forgets, to boast that in its inception it was "a thinking, not a trading community, the arena and mart for ideas." Nor did the Virginian settlers go to America merely for material gain.

America not a material-istic—

They were attracted by the romantic and
perilous enterprise of laying the foundation
of a new commonwealth across the sea; and
in their task they had the high hopes and
eager sympathy of those who remained in
Old England. Those settlers built up the
original States; and the blood of New
England flows in the veins of every State
to-day and largely determines the character
of the whole American people. The penetrat-
ing influence of the Puritan idealism is felt in
every part, and has been felt in every crisis,
of the national life.

It is the rare fortune of the American people
that in their formative days the quick moral
and religious life of the early communities left
on the larger life of the nation a deep impress
which has never been effaced, although, as
we have seen and yet shall see, the clear
lines of its beauty have been broken and
confused. By a process which has aptly
been compared to that of physical growth,
the living body of institutions, customs, duties
and privileges then created has made the
vital conditions of the national existence of
the present time. Now, as then, although
not as consciously as then, the American
people build upon the faith that God is
present in human life. Now, as then,

although not as generally as then, wealth is made the means of quickening the higher feelings and faculties. Now, as then, and now in clear recognition of the harder task than was then, the effort is made to guide life in clean and honest ways and consecrate intellectual as well as material resources to wise human ends. De Tocqueville regarded as the gravest danger that threatened a democracy, the ' complete absorption in the pursuit of material well-being and the means of material well-doing, to the disparagement and disregard of every ideal consideration. Shades of this prison-house constantly threaten to close in upon the growing nation. But America is not in bondage yet; and less, not greater, materialism has marked its recent years.

I shall be more restrained than Americans themselves in my criticism of American institu- tions. They are freer than Englishmen of the shallow official optimism that refuses to see self-defects and of the false patriotism that will not acknowledge such defects as refuse not to be seen. Their present temper even disposes them to excessive self-disparagement: and, indeed, a humble heart has always been beneath their bluster and brag. The loud depreciation of themselves that is, and the louder appreciation

—nor a braggart People.

of themselves that was, can be traced to a common root. It is easy to believe that, to wield any kind of influence over the masses of an enormous democratised community in whom ultimate power lies, an individual must make his expressed opinions much more pronounced than his inward convictions. Therefore, when the nation, after its first years of national inexperience, which were characterised by unreasonable optimism, was in danger of growing diffident in face of its great and increasing responsibilities and tasks, its leaders made conscious exaggeration, in order to maintain the nation in a just appreciation of its powers; and the people, slow to see through the exaggeration, were quick to make it their own, and then were inevitably driven to spend themselves that they might make sure of the wealth, and to throw themselves into violent motions that they might make sure of the powers, which they had been told that they possessed. By this process, without gaining the assurance that they sought, they lost the secret of silence, dignity and repose; and more than ever it seemed necessary, in order to impress the people, to resort to noise and effort, to act and effect. Then was the era of brag.

By reason of— But when, at last, the evils wrought by

the old exaggeration became apparent to a few, these, in order that they might be heard by the many, practised new exaggera- —new tions of speech and act in a direction opposite exaggera- to the old; and the unqualified denunciation of the ills of the body politic which have filled the land during recent years, and the spectacular legislative measures proposed as a remedy, have had so potent an effect upon the popular mind that, in America, bragging is in danger of becoming a lost art.   Two distinguished Oxford professors whom I met, one in New England and the other in California, said to me, in amazement and not without regret, that during many weeks spent in the country they had not heard a single brag. My experience has not been quite as happy as theirs, perhaps because I have gone farther afield; but candour compels me to say that, in America, I met fewer braggarts than I should have done had I been under the British flag, and that of "a certain condescension" I saw nothing at all.   For Americans are less disposed than Englishmen to dwell on and exaggerate their own national virtues, or to weigh them by the opposite vices of foreigners instead of by the virtues which those foreigners possess and they themselves lack.

—not
exces-
sive,—

"Boosters," indeed, afflicted me every day
—men, women, and children who have pledged
themselves to glorify their particular States
and towns in the hope of making, by calling,
them great. In the West, every town has its
"Boosters' Club" whose members wear a
conspicuous badge ; and every available adver-
tising spot is placarded with appeals to every
inhabitant to "Be a Booster"—and, if a boast
will help to boost, no good citizen will doubt
that the end will justify the means. In the
village of Pecatonica, Illinois, a man was
heard, and every other man there and in
every other American village, town or city
may any day be heard, solemnly declaring,
"This is the greatest city in the world"; and
on one occasion, when I foolishly attempted to
"boost" my own country as a colonising power,
I was told that, perhaps, there was a civilising
mission for England in such parts of the world
as America might not ultimately claim—and
the tone was as solemn, although not as
sincere, as that of a learned Brahmin in
Benares who once said to me that he was
willing to regard Jesus as an incarnation of
Vishnu for the benefit of the Western world.
But all this loud affirmation is always with
business intent and rarely without a saving
sense of humour. It is conscious and avowed;

it is naked and not ashamed. It indicates the essential vigour rather than the vanity of the social body. It shows that the people are progressing, but not fast enough to suit their desire. And, in the grateful sense of their exuberant youth, one forgets to be shocked by the lack of dignity, refinement and restraint which it displays. This is different from the national boasting with which America is universally charged and which, if it ever was, no longer is; and it is high time to drop the threadbare gibe that Americans are a braggart people.

The first settlers in America were brought —but face to face with an inspiring vision; their insufficient Self Con- hearts beat high with the hope of a new social fid. ʻ ʻe— order; they heard the challenge of liberty, equality and fraternity; and they flung themselves with transport into the new day which seemed to them to have dawned. And the remarkable achievements of the early Puritans were largely due to their sublime faith that New England was charged with the Divine mission to show the world what human society might be, when governed by constant devotion to the revealed law of God. Soon, shades of the prison-house closed in upon the growing nation. National experience, as was inevitable, modified the early faith; and the nation would be not less, but more, fitted for its eternal task if it were merely disciplined and chastened, and if, with the discovery that liberty is not a pastime, it had made the more important discovery that liberty has greater virtue and value on that account. But, in the difficulty and disaster of self-government, the splendid vision seems to have fled and to be discredited. I take, almost at random, an article on social and political conditions in one of the popular magazines, and in this sentence I find the present popular mood expressed: "The American people finds itself to-day in the position of a man with a dulled knife and broken cudgel in the midst of an ever-growing circle of wolves." This temper is far removed from the former national gaiety of heart which the nation, still young, ought still to possess and must regain if it is to overcome its confident internal foes. The worst cause conducted in hope is ever an overmatch for the noblest conducted in despondency ; and, if it could be done without impertinence, I should suggest to those public men who have the national welfare at heart that the fact that President Eliot of Harvard University, Miss Jane Addams of Chicago Hull House Settlement, and others who do not "lift up the voice or cry in the street," exert wide and profound

—the present Mood.

influence, indicates that America still has an ear to hear the still small voice when, by it, an enlightened conscience, an informed mind and a balanced judgment find expression in unexaggerated phrase.

CHAPTER II.

AMERICA AND ENGLAND.

" Strong Mother of a Lion-line
Be proud of these strong sons of thine
Who wrenched their rights from thee ! "—TENNYSON.

Democracy and elective Despotism—National Conservatism—
English Characteristics retained—Development of a new
human Type—The Master Force in American Civilisation
—Common Politeness—Sohrab and Rustum—English
Pride in American Achievements.

An
ominous
Lack—
LACK of democratic confidence shows itself, in America, in many ways, most obviously although perhaps not most significantly, in the growing fear of immigration to which I shall yet have occasion to refer. The race problem is, at bottom, a character problem. In the contact and conflict of different nationalities, the strongest life must ultimately prevail ; and the influx of foreign immigrants which now provokes alarm was hailed with joy when Americans were confident that the issue would be decided in their favour, as indeed it has hitherto been, by the superior quality of the native stock.

18

Still more ominous is the modern drift to —as at
what might be termed an elective despotism. Rome—
At New York and San Francisco, and at many
points between these geographical extremes,
Governors, Mayors and Commissioners have
been vested for a term of years with larger
powers than Englishmen would surrender to
any individual, however worthy, or to any
Commissioner, however carefully selected, even
for a day or an hour. "The cure of the ills of
democracy is more democracy" was once the
American shibboleth, but no one can or dares
pronounce it unfalteringly now; and, as the
machinery of democratic government, groaning
under the pressure of new demands, breaks
down in any of its parts, the attempt is made
to repair it, not by providing a more vital and
genuinely organised expression of the popular
will, but by giving to administrative officers more
and ever-increasing power, even as the Romans,
in similar stress, were wont to determine that
affairs required the direction of an absolute power
and would appoint a dictator by whom, with
steadiness and intrepidity, it should be exercised.

I attended a "town meeting," at Wellesley —of real
Hills, Massachusetts—a New England town. Democ-
As completely as in the ancient Greek City- racy.
State or in the modern Russian *mir*, pure
democracy was in action.   Every item of

business, great and small, all that might affect
in any degree any individual of the town, from
the appointment of executive officers to the
naming of streets, was submitted to the entire
body of the townsmen for decision by themselves. It was democracy as it once was
everywhere, and is now only here and there, in
this land. I should be the last man in the
world to suggest that no administrative act can
be truly democratic unless the people *en masse*
assemble to initiate and approve it. Such a
doctrine is both absurd in itself and the *reductio
ad absurdum* of government, as I heard the
President of Columbia University say in a
vigorous address to the University of California,
designed to prove that it is a false, spurious
and misleading democracy that would destroy
efficiency in working out the people's policies
by insisting that all the people shall join in
working them out. But that is also false
democracy which, from fear of the people,
surrenders popular rights to Commissioners
appointed by elected officials and placed beyond
popular control; and this is what is seen in
America to-day. Massachusetts will serve as
well as any other State to illustrate the im-
potence to which the people have been reduced.
Complaints were made of gross mismanage-
ment of the prisons of that State: for the press

A cure
that is—

in America retains its freedom of utterance,
even as did the tribune of the people at Rome
under the dictatorship appointed by the people
themselves.   But upon investigation it was
found that the prison Commissioners could not
be reached after their appointment except at
the trouble, expense and delay of judicial investigation; and nothing was done.   This system
gives great power without proper responsibility ;
it tends to remove the people's government
from the people's control; and it even fails to
secure efficiency.

Yet that, if it be a democracy at all, is —worse
democracy as it is in many cities, and is tending disease— than the
to become in all.   It is an attempt to cure
the ills of democracy by less democracy.   It is
adopted as a heroic remedy for the corruption
of the "political machine"; and for a time it
seems to succeed.   But this is mere seeming
and is but for a time.   The effect is analogous to
that sometimes seen in a sick man whose mind,
gaining increase of vitality from a new hope in
a fresh mode of treatment, sends a flush of
apparent life through the enfeebled body, even
while the mind collapses and death creeps on.
It is neither heroic nor remedial to disturb the
foundations of a temple in order to repair a
rat-hole in the wall; and it may be, as has been
suggested, that the corrupt politician, because

he is democratic in his methods, is on a more
ethical line of development than the modern
social reformer who attempts the new cure.

Retrospect and Prospect. This retrograde movement is likely to be
continued, at an accelerated pace, in the
immediate future, if only from fear of the
too forward movement of socialistic and other
schemes which the State fears. Americans are
impressionable and volatile and disposed to run
to extremes. They are quick to take up new
ideas and to carry them to their utmost extent.
They have not, nor could they have, the long
political experience which instinctively supplies
counterpoises to partial or novel impulses. It
may be that their crisp and varied climate
fosters nervous energy at the expense of
physical vitality and fits them for sharp rather
than sustained effort, for action rather than
endurance, for well-doing rather than patient
continuance in the same. In the long and
arduous task to which the American democracy
is committed, will the endurance of the future
equal the splendid energy of the past? That
is really the question that was raised by the
Secretary of State, Mr. Elihu Root, when he
recently impressed upon the students at Yale
University that, while democracy has proved
successful under simple conditions, it remains
to be seen how it will stand the strain of the

vast complication of life upon which the country
is now entering.

Of the answer, no one who knows the Origin-
American character can have serious doubt.
These movements which I have noted, greatly
as they have affected the surface of American
life, still remain superficial.   Americans, as
well if not as obviously as Englishmen, have
solidity, doggedness and tenacity—the qualities
that make them, as all competent observers
have found them, essentially conservative.
They are still, as they were described by Mr.
Bryce, like a tree whose pendulous shoots
quiver and rustle with the lightest breeze, while
its roots enfold the rock with a grasp which
storms cannot loosen.   America evinces its
English origin in nothing more clearly than in
a temper of mind at once courageous and
cautious, strong in serious hopes and free from
illusions, faithful to the best traditions of our
common forefathers yet not bound in subjection
to them but rather pressing forward to those
high ends towards which they and we work
together.   To meet difficulties as they arise
rather than by foresight, to learn by hard
experience rather than by reflection or pre-
meditation, to care more for dull precedents
than for brilliant intuitions, to make progress
by feeling a way softly step by step rather than

by projecting a way boldly with the easy assurance of abstract reasoners—these qualities with their defects, or these defects with their qualities are American, as well, although not as completely, as English traits.

-and
'evelop-
ent—
The American is, indeed, other than an Americanised Englishman. He is, as he claims to be, a new man. No one who has lived, as I have, in Australia and South Africa as well as in America, can fail to realise that the American, in a sense which does not apply to British colonists, has been made over into a new man by the new mode of life which he has embraced, and the new Government which he obeys, in his new land—a man who acts upon new ideas, new principles and new prejudices in the new world which he has made his own —a man in whom the climate and other potent factors of his new physical environment have wrought a new physiological type, while the more subtle influences of a new continent, which he has had almost to himself and in which he has long been kept practically free from contact and entanglement with the Old World, were producing a type intellectually and morally new.

-of
,mericans.
Yet the master-force in American civilisation has been, and is, the Anglo-Saxon spirit derived from the English settlers who colonised

the New World. The greatest migration of historic times has been to America from all the other nations of the world ; but the extreme preponderance of the English stock in America up to 1850 made a centre of influence that has proved irresistible in moulding into its likeness all subsequent settlers. Never was such an absorbing and transforming power as the English race domiciled in America, speaking the English language, possessing the English moral, legal and political ideals, and developing the precedents of English freedom. In consequence, the new American has the old English dislike of great schemes and of heroic remedies and of actions which are destructive of a complex civilisation ; and in America, as in England, freedom is broadening slowly down from precedent to precedent and will prove enduring because broad based upon the people's will. And now that America, like England, impelled by the *Zeitgeist*, greatest of all revolutionaries, whose force no bulwarks we may raise can resist, has been swept into the —asRoos general colonising movement from which she velt's r cent prai so long stood apart, and there has devolved of Englis rule in upon her as upon England, by an inevitable India indicates sequence of causes, responsibility to the national conscience and to history — the supreme earthly judge of human actions—for peoples in moral and political infancy, it is probable that a common task and common responsibilities will tend to fuller mutual comprehension and closer fellowship—perhaps even to conformity to a common type—of these two nations with whom the future of Imperial democracy now rests.

American Manners—A wit who does not lack wisdom has said that the English love Americans but not America, and the Americans love England but not the English; and I am afraid that I must testify to having discovered in many Americans a prejudice against me as an Englishman, which had to be overcome. It was not often made plain; for Americans take rank with the polite peoples of the world. They are not, indeed, as careful as Europeans, they are even much less careful than British colonists, to observe the gradations of conventional politeness according to rank, age and station; and I must confess that sometimes I have been foolishly disposed to resent a certain ease and familiarity of bearing and manner and tone on the part of men in positions which, being classified as "inferior" in other countries, are accepted there as involving an obligation of particular deference to the members of a "superior" class. But this pettiness passed as wider experience brought the discovery of a new and more genuine, because more inclusive, politeness: human and general, rather than individual and relative to persons. It may be that there is less courtesy in America than in Europe—that the æsthetic delicacy and distinction, the urbanity and suavity, all that makes the charm of the aristocratic cultivation of the Old World, is lacking in the New World. I do not dare to deny, and I do not need to assert this: have I not heard it asserted by Americans in New York and Chicago who are laboriously striving to create a society which shall have these inestimable qualities? But, certainly, common politeness, as I have said, is more human and general in America than in any other land. This is due to the wide, although, of course, far from universal, acceptance of personality as superior to all —mayketl the accessory attributes, such as rank and power American or even wealth, and as constituting what is man. essentially real and intrinsically valuable; so that to every person respect, and to all persons equal respect, is shown. This is the distinguishing feature of American life. It stamps the country as a democracy, in fact as well as in name; it makes it, what it calls itself, "God's Country," for the common man as also for the uncommon who remains sufficiently a man; and it gives an unquestionable sense of personal dignity and a distinction of personal bearing to the ordinary man.

But, in spite of the invariable politeness of Americans, some traces of their prejudice against Englishmen can be discerned. It has been created by a certain tone of superiority over Americans which Englishmen unconsciously, and therefore all the more impertinently and offensively, have assumed. But amongst all classes of Americans, not excluding even the Americanised immigrants from elsewhere than England, there exists a deep and noble desire which finds expression in many forms, sometimes pathetic but always dignified, that the Mother Country, whether or not she admires and loves, should know, understand and comprehend her offspring of the West. It may even be that some of the most hotly contested differences and disputes of America with England find an explanation in this desire: to use a poem of Matthew Arnold's by way of illustration, Sohrab challenges his father Rustum in the hope that, by some gallant action, he may be recognised as a worthy son. Few traces are now found of the habit, that once prevailed, of branding as servile and un-American the natural susceptibility, the English instinct, of a people of English descent. That habit grew patriotically out of old contentions with England, and politically out of a desire to conciliate the Irish-American vote. But there are some faults which require quiet and leisure for their growth and education ; and in America—it is one of the great compensations of her strenuous life—there is everything that can force a man out of a narrow sensitiveness, out of brooding thoughts, out of vanity and egotism. No American now thinks to prove the purity of his patriotism by flouting the land in which he has a legitimate right, or of spurning any of his just hereditary share in the great traditions of his ancestral country. And Englishmen are increasingly realising and taking parental pride, if not even claiming a parental share, in the achievements of the great and independent nation that has sprung from their loins. For myself, I confess that the achievements of Americans, when I reflect that they are those of my own race, quicken in me such intensity of feeling that I have consciously to strive constantly for the impartial mind, without which anything that I might write would be a tinkling cymbal, if it were not sounding brass.

CHAPTER III.

NATIVES AND ALIENS.

"But Thy most dreaded instrument
Is working out a pure intent."—WORDSWORTH.

A new Terminology—Its Significance—A prolific Race—Vital
Statistics — Reinforcement or Replacement?— The new
Alien—Heterogenity and Destiny—Heredity and Environ-
ment as Factors of Nationality—A grave Problem.

The old— WHEN travelling in India some years
ago, I discovered that, in order to
have a conscience void of offence towards
native Indians, it was necessary to address them
never as "natives," but always as "Indians,"
the former term, for obvious although incon-
clusive reasons, being held to imply a slight.
In America, however, in order to be all things
to all Americans, I found it expedient to style
them "natives," even those who had no strict
right to the term in which, in this instance,
a compliment is held to be implied. Those
who have been born in America are classified
as "native-born" and call themselves "natives,"
in distinction from aliens who were "foreign-

born." The natives proper, however, are the American Indians, all others being the descendants of comparatively recent immigrants; and the new terminology illustrates the extent to which Indians have passed out of, and immigrants have come into, the national consciousness.

The original proprietors and occupiers of —and the the New World were ever present to the mind new Native. of the original immigrants. They were only 250,000, all told; but they were settled where the new settlers wished to be—on the banks of rivers where, the land being fertile, their bread as well as their water was sure. Thus, the then immigrants were constantly face to face, often in hand-to-hand conflict, with the then natives who, relatively to the invaders, were a great multitude. There are still 250,000 Indians in America. But relatively to the 80,000,000 to which their supplanters have grown they are as nought; and, as they live in remote "Reservations" and are rarely seen by others than themselves, they are, by these others, forgotten or ignored. Thus the descendants and successors of the seventeenth-century immigrants have become the natives of to-day; and lo! the new native, who was the immigration problem to the Indian, finds the new immigrant a problem to himself.

I was told in England that I should be
amused in America by the incredible numbers
of the people who claim to be in direct line of
descent from the original English settlers ; and
I am not sure that I did not anticipate indulgence in some pleasantries at their expense.
But now that everywhere in America and
especially in New England I have found the
number of these claimants to be even greater
than I had been led to expect, I am not in-
credulous ; and therefore I am not amused and
have not one jest or gibe with which to enliven
this page. For the original colonists were,
beyond all precedent, a prolific race. They
numbered only 21,000 in the year 1640, when
increase by immigration practically ceased, not
to be resumed to any appreciable extent till
1830 ; yet between these years the population
grew, chiefly by natural increase, to nearly
13,000,000—a rate unparalleled in history, even
after allowance has been made for such immigration as was maintained. And comparatively recently it was estimated that, of the
entire population spread over the United States,
every third person could legitimately read in
the history of the first New England settlers
the history of his own progenitors. Were I an
American, I should, in the pride of lineage,
assume and maintain until it had been disproved

that I was included in the "every third";
unless, indeed, I claimed descent from the
settlers of Virginia, who did not, it is true, increase and multiply as mightily as the settlers in
New England, but who yet were not altogether
heedless of the invocation addressed to them
by the English poet Michael Drayton, who
bade them—

> ". . . in regions far,
> Such heroes bring ye forth
>   As those from whom we came ;
>   And plant our name
> Under that star
>   Not known unto our north."

In 1830 the new immigration, if it did not Vital Statistics.
then begin, did at least assume serious pro-
portions.   But where immigration abounded
population did not much more abound.   On the
contrary, in 1830 the rate of the natural increase
of population began to decline ; and ten years
later, in 1840, although during that period
2,500,000 aliens had come to America, the
total number of people in the country was no
greater, or greater by less than 10,000, than it
would have been without the immigrants if
only the previous rate of natural increase had
been maintained.   It is even claimed that
statistics show that this decline declared itself
first in those regions, in those States, and in
the very counties into which the foreigners

3

most largely entered; and the conclusion has
been drawn that by the great immigration the
native population has really been replaced by
the immigrants by whom it is generally supposed to have been reinforced.

An alien
Influence. To reckon up all the concurrent causes of
the decline of the native birth-rate at that time,
it would be necessary to write the economic
and social history of the American people
during several decades—a task which is as
far above my abilities as it is beyond my
present scope. I understand, however, that
ordinarily population increases inversely to
its density, and that therefore the influx of
2,500,000 aliens, congested in towns as they
were apt to be, may well have been one of
the factors in the decline. But, on the other
hand, if the aliens had not come, and if, as is
contended would have been the case, an equal
or greater number of natives had therefore
been born, these would have increased the
density, and then would have diminished the
subsequent increase, of population. It may,
however, be fairly contended that, in this latter
case, the decrease would have been less than
it actually has been. The aliens emphasised
social distinctions, and the social factor is as
powerful as the economic in determining the
rate of population; and in a community which

has groups with different social standards, prudential restraint, if practised at all, will be exercised by the group which has the standard to maintain. The natives, not the aliens, were that group.

The aliens, doubtless, both reinforced and replaced. And at that period reinforcement was a necessity, while such replacement as occurred was even less serious in its effect than in its extent. For immigration then, was chiefly of races which, in habits, institutions and traditions, were kindred to the original colonists; and down to 1875 no other immigration was sufficiently numerous to have any effect on the national characteristics. A minister of religion in the Mid-West, writing of his pastoral work, records that he would in one day eat breakfast with a brawny Canadian, visit a school taught by a Frenchman, call on a district director who spoke the dialect of Hans Breitman, and take supper with an Englishman who said, after the fashion of his native Warwickshire, "not far from we." The next day, he would take his morning meal with a Scotch-Irishman, visit a school taught by a lady from Alabama, receive a call from a district officer who was once a Welsh sea-captain and remained a Welshman, inquire the way of a Dane, and, losing it, soon inquire

Immigration Statistics

again of a Swede, and finally would sleep with a New York politician. All those foreigners were his racial kinsmen; and their minister reports that easily and speedily they were transformed to the American type. But since 1875, there has been a change which an increasing number of thoughtful Americans contemplate with grave misgivings. Last year 1,200,000 aliens settled in America—the largest number ever received by any, even by this, country in a single year. And whereas in 1865, 56 per cent. of the immigrants came from Great Britain and Ireland, 32 per cent. from Germany, and 2 per cent. from Scandinavian countries—that is, 90 per cent. from the Teutonic group—and only a fraction of 1 per cent. each from Austria-Hungary, Italy and Russia, the proportion last year was 13 per cent. from Great Britain and Ireland and 6 per cent. from Scandinavian countries, while 27 per cent. came from Austria-Hungary, 22 per cent. from Italy, and 18 per cent. from Russia.

National Ties.

These immigrants provide cheap labour and are found everywhere, although especially in large cities, doing "menial" work which, being restricted to aliens, has, even in this democracy, come into some contempt. It is curious to hear, in the Northern States, arguments for the introduction of immigrants that were used in the Southern States for the introduction of negro slaves; and just as in the South, owing to the negroes there, one race has withdrawn itself, socially and politically, from the other, so in the North, owing to the immigrants there, society is beginning to experience a social stratification which is tending to break up its former homogeneity. There are, indeed, in America little Russias, little Italys, little Syrias, and great Jerusalems—vortex rings of nationality—closed to the outside medium in which they live; and the remarkable American-ising process, of which I have spoken, has had its best results, it must be confessed, rather in opening fuller intercourse within these several racial groups than in relating them to the American element in the popula-tion, so that America, politically a federal union, is tending to be that also in its racial character and its type of civilisation. Now, a State is strong in proportion to the number of ties operating to hold it together; and the great natural ties are community of race, of language, of religion and of sentiment or historical association. In Australia I once heard a clergyman impress upon his congrega-tion that, taking history as a whole, the nations which have left the greatest mark in religion, art and literature, such as Judæa, Greece, Rome, England, Germany and France, were, at the time of their greatness, essentially homogeneous; and Australians, with rare exceptions, believing that national decadence has always followed the mixture or dispersal of races, concur in, or rather compel, legislation which is intended to exclude foreigners from the Commonwealth. Americans, however, have long held that their country proves its greatness by the presence within it of so many diverse races, and that by the ultimate result of these multitudinous factors the national greatness will be enhanced. But, within recent years, this assurance has become less sure; and I have met many Americans who fear that, by the great increase of foreign immigrants of all nationalities, there may have been a distinct lessening of the national powers of cohesion and resistance, through the weakening of the ties by which alone great aggregations of human beings can be bound together in a State.

The old and the new Immigrants.

The new immigrants differ, not to their advantage, from the old in respect of physique and personal qualities as well as in racial type. Previously the physical discomforts, the hard labour, and the isolated lives that immigrants had to endure in America deterred such as were not vigorous, ambitious and alert; but now the alien goes as an adventurer eager to take advantage of a widely-heralded national prosperity in which, he is led to believe, he can easily share. Fifty years ago, when it required energy, prudence, and foresight to accumulate the necessary means to cross, and to find the way across, the Atlantic, it was a rightful presumption regarding the average immigrant that he was amongst the most thrifty members of the nation, whichever it was, from which he came. But to-day, as was pointed out by the late Dr. Francis A. Walker when he was Superintendent of the United States' census, this presumption is completely reversed—"so thoroughly has the Continent of Europe been crossed by railways, so effectively has the business of emigration been exploited, that it is now amongst the least thrifty and prosperous members of any European community that the emigration agent finds his best recruiting ground."

In Italy, Germany, France and Russia, even in the remotest corners of these countries, I myself, although merely a tourist in them, have met steamship emigration agents. In Europe they are a great army: the Red Star Line alone had at one time no less than 1500 agents. And in America itself I found that

the steamship companies have their agents
whose business it is to persuade immigrants
already in the country to take out prepaid
passages for their relatives, friends and acquaintances still in Europe; and these agents
are so successful that 50 per cent. of recent
immigrants have been "prepaids." It is true
that aliens, before being allowed to settle in
the country, are examined by medical officers ;
but minor physical defects, of which 26,424
were reported in 1905, do not exclude ; and,
in spite of admitted laws of heredity, those
who, having no definite disease, such as
trachoma or mental abnormality, are yet reported as of poor physique, have no "certifi-
cate of disability" returned against them, if
only some citizen offers a guarantee that they
will not become a public charge. And in this
connection it is significant that, during the
first three months of 1906, when 23,733
children in New York schools were medically
examined, of 17,362 of these who were declared
to be suffering from some physical abnormality,
20 per cent. were of foreign birth, and the rest
of the defectives, although they were born in
the country, bore names that gave evidence of
foreign parentage ; and of 88 children examined
in one "truant school," 77 were declared defectives, and of these 74 were of foreign birth.

And the New York State Lunacy Commissioners reported in 1904 that, of all the insane patients in New York City, 60 per cent. were foreign-born.

Many of the new immigrants have been under Governments encrusted with age-long despotism, corruption and inefficiency. They *Moralist versus Statistician.* therefore come to America with little or no training in constructive citizenship, often without even elementary education, and having a lower economic standard than that which prevails here. They necessarily lack the political capacity acquired by native Americans from several centuries of self-government in the American Colonies and in the United States, and inherited from centuries of political growth in England before the colonisation of America. That all Governments are necessarily bad is an assumption that has grown into their tissues and become indurated. Compulsion has bred in them perverse stubbornness; and prohibition has developed strong desire for all forbidden fruit. Sophocles said of Æschylus that he did right, all unaware of it. It is much easier to reach the other habit; and many immigrants, doubtless, do wrong by mere momentum of acquired conditions. And as institutions and beliefs are seen to lend strength to each other, the teeth that are set

on edge against American institutions are easily
brought to gnash at American beliefs. Hence,
attacks on religion, patriotism and the family
by immigrants are sometimes heard ; and the
most violent and extreme Socialist and Anarchist
agitators, of whom I have met not a few, are
comparatively recent immigrants whose habits
of thought and emotional attitude have been
acquired in the countries from which they have
come. The tendency of Americans to des-
potise their institutions while optimistically
holding that they retain their original democracy,
seems to be largely due to a sense of need to
control the dissident elements introduced by immigration. And many thoughtful Americans are
found who ask whether national industrial prosperity is not being purchased at too high a price
if, on the one hand, there is a progress of things,
while on the other there is a decline of souls
—if, while the statistician registers a growing
progress, the moralist detects a gradual decline.

A grave   In view of all these facts, this other fact is
Problem.   of supreme significance. According to the
Census Bulletin No. 22, the decrease in children
born of native parents between 1890 and 1900
was 13 per 1000, while during the same period
the increase of children of foreign-born parents
was 44 per 1000. Mr. R. R. Kuczynski, after
careful study of the population statistics of

Massachusetts, concludes that, even in that New England State, "the native population is dying out." If that is the case, then the people who supplanted the Indians are themselves being supplanted by the immigrants. And many do seriously apprehend that Americans, in becoming a cosmopolitan people, are ceasing to have a distinct national type. I, for my part, although by no means insensible of the deep and universal upheaval that has been involved in the incoming of these millions of immigrants, am still convinced, from my observation of natives and aliens during the months that I was in close personal contact with them in all parts of the country, that the foundations of American thought, religion, character and type remain unimpaired. The country is, indeed, heterogeneous in the composition of its population; yet the English tongue and the English tradition overbear all competitors, reconcile in themselves all rivalries, and sustain themselves in directive control, modified, of course, but not weakened, by the variety of foreign influences to which they are subjected. Doubtless here, as elsewhere, I am making an inference vastly disproportioned to the facts observed; but, equally doubtless, others whose conclusions are other than mine are doing the same.

Congeni-
ality as a
national
bond.

To my mind, the force and effect of American life and American institutions is one of the most extraordinary phenomena of all history; and I find myself less sceptical than many Americans in regard to the power of American democracy to persist and prevail by transforming its aliens into natives, in fact as well as in name, by the new social and political responsibilities which are immediately laid upon them, and by which, almost from the day of their arrival, they are involved in a new scheme of ethical incentive and constraint. A bond of nationality, as strong even as that of community of blood, is found in acceptance, inbred if not inborn, of the same political ideas, fundamental laws and habits of thought, which regulate the relations and intercourse between man and man and constitute congeniality; and when to these a common tongue is added, an environment is created which, perhaps, does more to promote unity than it is in the power of kinship alone to effect. Yet no one who grasps with the moral imagination the prospective as well as the immediate bearings of the facts which confront this nation could fail to recognise that a grave problem is created by the presence of these millions—since 1850, 21 millions—of people who have come from all parts of the earth, sprung from all races, speaking all languages, believing all religions and bringing with them all kinds of inherited characteristics and tendencies, and who have already created a cosmopolitan and complicated life hitherto un-equalled in any land.

CHAPTER IV.

THE MAKING OF AMERICANS.

"A strange harmonious inclination
Of all degrees to reformation."—HUDIBRAS.

A Russian Reminiscence—An American Phrase and Passion—
Compassion or Justice?—The Alien's Case—Immigration
and national Consolidation—*Stasis*—An Italian Debate—
The Americanising Process—New economic Conditions.

The
Fruit—

I HAPPENED to be in Russia, some years
ago, during a time of severe famine when,
from many foreign countries, contributions
were sent to aid in the relief of the starving
peasantry. I was then profoundly impressed
by the generosity of America, whose gift
greatly exceeded that of all other nations
combined; and, in a hasty generalisation, I
concluded that Americans were, of all peoples,
the most compassionate. On my arrival in
America, I seemed to find further evidence of
this characteristic in the large hospitality which
has been accorded to the millions of aliens,
multitudes of them Russians, who have taken

46

refuge in the country from the economic and political stress which they had endured in their native lands.

But beneficence has not always its roots in benevolence; and, on closer scrutiny of the unquestionable generosity of Americans, I am disposed to ascribe it to some other, not necessarily less noble, motive than pity. I should indeed hesitate to say that Americans are, of all peoples, the least compassionate; but I should hesitate still more to include compassion in any catalogue of their characteristics.

The American character is the result of a great ideal untiringly pursued—the ideal of moral order founded on respect for self and for others, that is, on personal dignity and worth. Their very religion has dignity rather than humility as its note; and their spiritual teachers rarely press upon their attention those dark and stubborn facts of human nature by which the insignificance of man and of all human achievements might be recalled. In compassion, there is something which looks like weakness in those who are subject to it, and which seems to impute weakness to those who are its object—a weakness twice cursed, cursing those who give and those who take. Therefore, in this prosperous and robust

—and the Root—

people there is a perceptible tendency to
contemn compassion, and the very word
charity is to them taboo.

—and the
Soil—

From their insistence upon personal worth
and dignity as inhering in every human being,
irrespective of all accessory attributes, they
have acquired a fine sense of what is due to
themselves and what they owe to others; and
their generosity proceeds from this sense of
justice rather than from the sentiment of
compassion.   To give a square deal is an
American phrase and an American passion.
At the time of the Russian famine to which I
have referred, America enjoyed unprecedented
prosperity, and the traditional friendship of
Russia towards America was a phrase on
every lip; and Americans felt that they owed
it to Russia and still more to themselves to
give liberally of their abundance for Russians'
relief.

Even in social settlement work, in which,
if in anything, pity might be thought to find
expression, it is disavowed as a principle of
action.   Mr. Robert A. Woods, the Warden
of the South End House in Boston, explicitly
says that the sentiment of pity and mercy
as a motive of social service has become
outworn.   The new motive, he declares, is
"a certain spirit of moral adventure, carrying

a suggestion of statesmanship"—a motive which certainly is not mortifying to human pride, but which, from close observation of settlements in Boston and elsewhere in America, I should agree with Mr. Woods in determining as the motive that prevails. And if it should be said that social service from such a motive is the perfection of selfishness, I should reply that it at least approximates to the selfishness of the perfect man who recognises that the good of others is his good, and that the way to do self the highest service is to serve the race.

It is, therefore, not to imply a reproach that I insist that it was not because Americans were touched with the feeling of the infirmities of the immigrants that these have been freely admitted to America and to all the privileges of American citizenship. To have denied them hospitality would have been to put an indignity upon them and would have been incompatible with the dignity of America. America, therefore, owed it to herself and to them that they should be received. And the welcome extended to them was certainly not made less cordial by the general belief, "carrying a suggestion of statesmanship," that, in addition to the benefits accruing to the immigrants, the economic and political

—of American Generosity—

4

effect of their settlement in America involved an increase of the national population, prosperity, power and prestige.

—towards Immigrants.

Of recent years, however, as I have said, it has been contended by many, and the conviction is spreading, that the aliens have weakened, not strengthened, the nation; and evidence accumulates every day that the nations from which they have come have been weakened by their emigration—Sweden and Italy, for example, have admitted, even officially, that they propose, in self-preservation, to use every legitimate means, not only to prevent further emigration, but even to induce as many as possible of their countrymen now settled in America to return to their native lands which have been depopulated to an alarming extent and are in actual want of able-bodied men. Should this ever become the national conviction in America, immigration would be discouraged as heartily as it has hitherto been encouraged, and from the same motive of equal justice to herself and to foreign States. The American people, in judicial mood, will hear the case against the immigrants and will seek to do justice, however much mercy may be loved.

Revised Statistics.

Judicially, therefore, should the case be stated. And in the first place, to this end, immigration statistics should be revised. The number of immigrants is not as great as is made to appear. Before 1856, no distinction was made, in statistical returns, between travellers and immigrants. Even now, although it is known that so many foreign-born American citizens return—as many as 500,000 have been known to return, in a period of two months—temporarily to their native lands, that at certain periods of the year the efflux is greater than the influx, no effort is made to deduct from the annual immigration returns the numbers of those who have been counted in previous years. Nor is due account taken of other important factors. The stream of immigration, even at the highest estimate of its volume, is small, relatively to the river into which it flows; the annual number of aliens rarely exceeds 1 per cent. of the receiving native population; moreover, the aliens migrate, not in organised communities but as families, or still more frequently as individuals, and are thus more easily dominated and Americanised than they could otherwise be, the mass of transforming power being increased every year by the conquest of newcomers.

The charge against the immigrants which I have heard most frequently and most vehe- A Charge against Immigrants—

mently urged is that, owing to the diversities of race, language and religion which they have introduced to the body politic, they have broken up the national unity and seriously impaired the national powers of cohesion and resistance. I have already stated that I found little Italys, little Syrias, little Germanys, and great Jerusalems in America; and certainly it is unsatisfactory that these aliens should be as isolated from each other and from the native population as I have shown them to be. But there is another and larger fact which ought to be fully recognised and frankly admitted in every discussion of this feature of our problem. During the years of unrestricted immigration, America has been steadily advancing towards, not receding from, substantial unity in all its parts.

—disproved by—

When all Americans were the direct descendants of the English colonists of the seventeenth century, there were several groups of communities, such as the New England group, the Middle group (New York, New Jersey and Pennsylvania), and the Southern group (Maryland, Virginia, Georgia and the Carolinas), each of which was practically a little nation differing from all the others in spirit, in opinions, in social usages and in laws, and was unsympathetic and sometimes even unfriendly to them. Then it was that there was no cohesive principle, no centralising life; and in 1765, at the assembly at New York of the first Continental Congress, the delegates from the several colonies "like Ambassadors from remote nations, could at first only stare at one another as utter strangers in face, in character, even in manner and speech." This provincialism of the several States is rapidly dying out, if it is not already dead. America is, and acts as, a nation. The separate States are freely committing themselves to the national idea and to the central Government. Sectional lines and differences are being rapidly eliminated. The old claims of separate States' rights, or at least the claims of separate selfish States' interests, are being voluntarily abandoned. Mr. Elihu Root, Secretary of State, without provoking serious protest from any quarter, recently raised the issue which was that of the Civil War, when, on December 12, 1906, he said that, if the several States did not exercise in due measure the powers reserved to them by the Constitution "a construction of the Constitution will be found to vest the power in the central Government." Immigrants have not seriously interfered with the operation of the great laws governing national growth and development in centralisa-

—Quotation from M. C. Tyler's History of American Literature

tion, consolidation and union ; rather, they
have themselves been caught in the sweep
of this tremendous cohesive and centripetal
force, and America to-day, as never before, is
one people, united in spirit, in thought, in
purpose and in act.   The majority of the
"aliens" are even *plus Américains que les
Américains*;   and   the   Jews   of   America,
relatively to their number, contributed the
greatest proportion of volunteers to fight for
America during the Spanish-American war.

The
American-
ing
Process—
Every day, as I ploughed my furrow of
inquiry, I turned up new evidence of the
unprecedented absorbent power of the
American people by which, of all the diverse
elements pouring into their country, one new
nation has been made. I met recent immigrants, some of them Russian Jews whom I
had known in their native land ; and in many
instances it seemed to me that their fibre,
their tissue, the convolutions of their brain,
their very nerve fluid had been changed by
the genial and potent influence of American
national life—even in external appearance
they were transformed.   Even before the
immigrants reach America the Americanising
process begins through the imagination—that
strange source of all human progress—which
has been profoundly affected by all that they

have read or heard of the New World; and no one could ever forget, who had ever seen, the rapt expression on the face of an immigrant when from the steamer as it enters New York Harbour—

"Unde totam licet aestimare Romam"—

he catches his first glimpse of the Statue of Liberty which he had heard of and read of and seen pictures of and dreamed of and almost worshipped in his far-off home in the Old World. Even the stars in their courses fight for America, if not always for the immigrant when he lands. The politicians would fain prevent his assimilation in order that his vote might be easily manipulated by them; but first of all he must have a vote to be handled, and to this end the politicians provide him with naturalisation papers, fraudulently it may be—the State superintendent of elections in New York estimates that 100,000 fraudulent naturalisation papers were issued in New York State alone in 1903. Thus at the very beginning of his life in America the immigrant feels himself identified with, and takes delight and pride in, the American name and nation; and lo! already the alien is bound to the native by the tie of a common sentiment, the ἦθος of the Greeks, which is one of the most powerful factors of nationality.

Of course, there are large exceptions to be made. A battery current flowing through some metals disintegrates, although in others it molecularly reforms, their substance; and the thrill of new experiences rouses in many immigrants, and shocks them into conformity with, base passions rather than noble aspirations—is to them a savour of death unto death and not of life unto life, according to the eternal law. Finding themselves equal in one thing— equally free and privileged under the law— with all American citizens, they come to regard themselves as equal in all other respects. Having left behind them conventional inequalities, arbitrary privileges and historical injustice, they go still further in their new environment and rebel against the inequalities of merit and virtue, of capacity and wealth. Beginning with a just principle, they develop it into an unjust one; and instead of the thraldom of the traditional from which they have escaped, they subject themselves to the more unwholesome thraldom of the novel, which is none the less dangerous because it disguises itself under the fiction of emancipation. This is the real origin and fountain-head of that peril to a State which Aristotle in his *Politics* calls *stasis*—the assumption and assertion of a distinct position in the State, with malicious intent towards another party in it, from which arises "a want of justice and proportion in their aims, leading to contempt of moral goodness and of intellectual worth, and sometimes to harsh treatment of old families and confiscation of their properties."

In Boston, a few weeks after my arrival in America, I attended a debate between Italians upon Socialism *versus* Anarchy. Undeniably there was abundant evidence of *stasis*. The fiercest attacks upon American institutions provoked the warmest applause; and the meeting was roused to a high pitch of enthusiasm by a fiery orator who roundly declared that in America there was less liberty, equality and fraternity than in any country of the Old World. An estimable American, whose literary work is neither unknown nor unappreciated in England, was in the chair, and invited me, who might be presumed to be impartial, to take part in the debate; and I made such defence of American institutions as I could, by simply comparing them with corresponding institutions in Russia. But the Italians, so far from being convinced, became still more extravagant in their denunciations; and the meeting broke up in confusion, to the accompaniment of wild cheers, when one of them hotly proclaimed himself an Anarchist and

—as illustrated at Boston—

advocated "the use of chemicals as in Russia
to rid the country of capitalists, politicians and
even the President, who are worse despots and
bureaucrats than the Tsar and his officials ever
dared to be." This seemed to me a most
serious symptom at the time; but I see it in
its proper perspective now. The debate was
conducted in Italian, and I did not then
appreciate the significance of that fact. It
meant that those Italians were recent immigrants; for all others have learned, and prefer,
even in private and much more in public, to
use the English tongue. Undoubtedly, the
tendency of the alien to violent socialistic and
anarchistic denunciation is in inverse proportion to the amount of liberty he has enjoyed
before he went to America; but, equally undoubtedly, this tendency decreases in direct
proportion to the length of time that he lives
in his new country and the extent to which he
mingles with and becomes part of the community. And although I have met and been
in intimate relations with multitudes of immigrants, I have found in the ranks of the
Socialists and Anarchists few citizens who
were of the second generation of aliens and
thus had taken in the impressions and influences of American life and education during
the impressionable period of childhood. Wood-

–but tri-
mphant.

bine, in New Jersey, is a township of Russian Jews, few if any others than the public-school teachers being Gentiles. Yet even there, where Americanising influences might be supposed not to predominate, I found that Socialist and Anarchist aliens quickly shed their peculiar tenets as they discover that in America the very premises of their arguments are lacking—the political repression, the crushing weight of an enormous military system, the career closed to the talent of the poor, and the system of profound social inequality. And, although there can easily be detected amongst the immigrants an element of social unrest, this comes out of their hopes, and not, as it did in their native lands, out of their fears, and may therefore be regarded without fear.

Were I an American who had reached these conclusions regarding the effects of immigration upon the national life, I should not therefore be inclined to rank myself among the advocates of a policy of *laisser faire*. That the present has not been irreparably injured by the past does not give any guarantee that the future can be safely left to take care of itself. Except within restricted areas which are becoming narrower every year, America has not the former conditions of life or the former kinds of work to offer the immigrant who now finds in

The Past and the Future.

his New World many of the conditions which
drove him from the Old World; and, in proportion as America, in its economic structure,
grows into resemblance to the older civilisa-
tions, it necessarily loses, and in some
measure it has already lost, its capacity to
transmute the baser elements of those countries which, hitherto, it has received, with
great advantage to most of them and without
irreparable disaster, perhaps even not without
great advantage, to itself.

CHAPTER V

THE JEWS.

Templar.
"I've nothing against Nathan, I am angry
With myself only.

Saladin
And for what?

Templar.
For dreaming
That any Jew could learn to be no Jew—
For dreaming it awake.

Saladin.
Out with this dream."—LESSING.

Polygenous and Judaic New York—Israel in Russia—The
Exodus—*For the Children's Sake*—Yiddish Plays—The
Americanised de-Judaised Jew—A comprehensive Curse—
The real Hebrew Heart—Redintegration of Jews and
Judaism.

NEW YORK, even during its ante-natal A Micro-
existence as New Amsterdam was a
community of many tongues, many customs
and many faiths, and had within and near its
confines a population speaking eighteen different
languages. When it ceased to be Dutch and,
becoming English, came to be New York, it
remained hospitable to men of all races and

was recognised as "the most polygenous of all the British dependencies in North America." Now that it is neither Dutch nor English, it is still conspicuously cosmopolitan ; and to-day New York, more than any other city that is or ever was, offers new and varied exemplifications of the age-long, world-wide problem of the contact of diverse races of men. The city is a microcosm. Its European groups nearly correspond, numerically to the relative populations, and geographically to the relative positions, of their respective nations in the Old World ; and in addition to this miniature Europe in New York, there are representative groups from all other continents of the globe. Here, the immigration problem assumes its gravest and acutest form ; and my original impression could find no more apt expression than in a sentence, itself a problem, which was wrung from an American author of the seventeenth century by the vexed question of that time :—

"If the whole conclave of hell can so compromise exadverse and diametrical contradictions as to compolitise such a multimonstrous maufrey of heteroclites and quicquidlibets quietly, I trust I may say with all humble reverence they can do more than the Senate of Heaven."

Of all the "maufrey" of immigrants, Jews *Russian* are held to be the most "multimonstrous" as *Jews.* they certainly are the most multitudinous ; and as Jews, especially from Russia, are flowing into America, and especially into New York, in a stream of rapidly increasing volume, this chapter upon the Jews in America will treat chiefly of the Russian Jews in New York— that most Christian city whose every fifth inhabitant is a Jew—who will be the deter- mining influence on Judaism in, and of Judaism on, this New World.

The Russian Pale, which was created in *A new* 1843, includes the old kingdom of Poland and *Exodus.* the north-west provinces of Russia which originally belonged to Poland. The Jews in this vast territory number only about 5,000,000 in a total population of about 42,500,000 ; but as they are not allowed to own or cultivate land, they necessarily crowd into and congest the towns. There, some acquire wealth which procures protection ; but multitudes are huddled together in poverty and fear, borne down in the press and strife for existence— a despised and persecuted race. Ragged, half- fed, crushed mortals, without any hope of rising out of their misery so long as they re- main within the Pale beyond which, in Russia, they may not go, they yet are saved from

utter despair by the faith which they cherish
with religious fervour and, in religious phrase,
express—the faith that the justice and mercy
which they find not in the Russians whom
they have seen are, perchance, in the Americans whom they may one day see, and are
certainly and eternally, in spite of outward
seeming, in their Unseen Jehovah, by Whom,
in token thereof, in the holy place of His
Temple, the Law and the Mercy Seat were
enshrined.   This faith is kept alive by letters
which they receive from their sons and
daughters and from friends and acquaintances
in America and which are sometimes read
aloud in the synagogues, testifying to a reasonable chance, even for Jews, a chance of getting
a fair start in life and of rising above poverty,
degradation and shame in a land where

> "Men live in a grander way
> With ampler hospitality."

A greater Jerusalem.   The voyage across the sea seems to these
modern Jews no less hazardous a venture than
their fathers' journey through the wilderness;
but they commit themselves to the Divine
guidance and protection, and journey—a great
host—to their new land of promise which
already has 15 per cent. of the Jews of the
world, who are only one-half of 1 per cent. of

the population of the world, and which has, in New York alone, 800,000 members of this race —a greater number than ever before was gathered together in one place, even in Jerusalem in her palmiest days. How, then, do they fare? Do they find at last a home? Or are they still strangers and wanderers as all their fathers were?

One morning, during my residence in the University Settlement in New York, in the heart of the Ghetto, as I was strolling along the Bowery, I saw two Jewish children, both bonnie bairns, eagerly scanning a poster at the door of a Jewish theatre. Many people, Jews without exception, were pressing in, and the faces of the children showed that they had the desire but not the means to join them. In spite of the Yiddish jargon in Hebrew characters on the placard, I read the announcement of a *matinée* "for the children's sake"; and I offered to pay these children's way. They accepted on condition that I should get their parents' consent and should go to the entertainment with them—a prudent and proper precaution on their part. The parents neither spoke nor understood English, but I mustered up enough Russian to convey my request; and when they learnt that I was living in the Settlement they accepted me as

For the Children's Sake.

5

tchestnie tchelovek, an honourable man, and proved their confidence in me by giving permission to others of their children than those whom I had invited to gō to the theatre with me. I was, I believe, the only *Shaigatz* (that is, Gentile), and my companions were the only children, there. My little knowledge of Yiddish had proved a dangerous thing: the title, not the intention, of the entertainment was *For the Children's Sake*. I had expected a pantomime; but it was a tragedy of Jewish life in New York that had been advertised, and the children showed appalling familiarity with the scenes that were depicted on the stage and gravely assured me, out of their own experience, that it was a very realistic play. We were first transported to Russia where we found several parents discussing letters which they had received from America, and heard them resolve to emigrate there—for the children's sake. We came to America with a band of immigrants and settled in New York. There we saw the children becoming Americanised in speech, in manner and in dress, but becoming also de-Judaised in religion and morals—losing their own souls while they gained the world. And, finally, we beheld the parents heartbroken over the disastrous results of their experiment and heard them resolve to return to poverty and persecution in Russia—for the children's sake.

I have seen many Yiddish plays since then, Children and Parents Israel. most of them mere sketches, bits of local colour or broad patches of caricature; and although few of them express the deepest characteristics of the Americanised Jews, or grasp more than what is exotic and superficial in them, yet it is not without significance that all the characters in the end come to actual or constructive grief owing to the disintegrating and demoralising effect of their new environment. And now that I have had some insight into the lives and longings of this people, their secret sorrows and joys, their many shortcomings and crimes, and the meaning of them all, I can say, with my little Jewish friends, that these are very realistic plays. Of course, I have seen much else than the plays present. Much else is apparent on the surface, and is the first that all, and all that most, observers ever see; and there is general complacency on the part of native Americans as they regard the Americanised Jews in their midst.

I have heard the voice of Israel's Their bitter cry discontent in Russia, the gathering stir and tumult of its restlessness there; but I have found beneath the surface of the Ghetto of New York, as deep a storm and stress of

human life, and as intense a ferment of feeling, as is to be found in the Russian Pale. I
have heard Jews curse America as deeply as
ever, even by Jews, Russia was cursed. A
prominent Jew, who has spent his life in the
interests of his race, has told me, and I have
heard Mr. Zangwill report, that the elders in
Israel curse Columbus for having discovered
America, the land to which they came and
from which, renouncing all its opportunities
of material gain, they would gladly go to
Russia again, with their children, for the
children's sake, were it not that, owing to
the Russian closed door, they themselves
cannot go back although they would, and
that, owing to the open doors in America,
their children would not go back if they could.
One old Orthodox Russian Jew I met who
had resolved to return to his native village,
at the peril of his life. In America, he had
found nothing to love during the years he
had dwelt in the land; and in the hour of
leaving it forever, his one regret was that his
children and grandchildren remained, at the
peril of their souls. At the Jews' domestic
celebrations of the Passover Feast the eldest
son represents Elijah, who is supposed to
appear and renew the Messianic hope.
America needs the immediate fulfilment of

the prediction of the Book which Gentiles and Jews alike revere: "I will send you Elijah the prophet, . . . and he shall turn the heart of the fathers to the children and the heart of the children to the fathers, lest I come and smite the earth with a curse."

In Russia there are many Jews who live beyond the Pale—merchants of the first guild; professional men with university degrees; students in institutions of higher education; surgeons, apothecaries and dentists; and skilled artisans who are members of their respective trade guilds. These are free to go to America and would make admirable immigrants; but most of them remain away, despite the prejudice that prevails against them in Russia. They have fuller information than their brethren in the Pale regarding the dangers to faith and morals to which Jews are exposed, as well as the opportunities of work and wealth which they have, in America; and having with all Jews, along with their hard grip of the things of the world and their carefulness in a bargain, a just estimate of the limited value of earthly possessions, and esteeming their faith more than gold or comfort or respectability or even life, they deem it nobler, for the children's sake, to bear the ills they have in Russia

Russian Pale and America Ghetto.

than to fly to those in America of which they know.

A Yiddish
Play,
wherein
to catch—
There is a play by an Americanised Russian Jew, Gordin, whom I met in New York, which may help us here—*Gott, Mensch und Teufel.* It is crude in conception and execution, yet it is more than a mere transcript of observation—is indeed, in spite of its obvious resemblance in theme and treatment to the Book of Job, more nearly an original composition than any other Yiddish play that I have seen. In it, as in the sacred Book, Satan appears as a moral and religious censor of the human race; but, whereas Job is an Eastern Emir of large possessions and a non-Israelite, the central figure of the modern play is a Jewish scribe who earns no more than a few hundred dollars a year as a copyist of the law. Poverty tested Job in his Eastern world; but in America prosperity is perilous to the Jew. Accordingly, in the Prologue of *God, Man and Devil,* when Jehovah directs the attention of Satan to the faith and zeal of the Scribe, the Adversary replies that it is easy for a Jew to be pious when he is poor, but were this one made rich he would curse God to His face. Authority to enrich and so to tempt the Servant of the Lord is given to Satan, who meets his first difficulty in the

refusal of the Scribe to accept proffered wealth, which has no attraction of any kind for him. But possession no less than prohibition may awaken desire ; and when at last the Scribe allows a lottery ticket to be left on his table, the Arch-Tempter knows that he has gained his immediate end. *Ce n'est que le premier pas qui coûte;* and Satan now has an easy task. Of course, the Scribe wins a prize, and the money which comes to him seems great wealth ; but its possession, so far from sating, stimulates his lust for gold, and soon seven other devils worse than the first find place in his heart, which, until his affliction by prosperity, had been "holy unto the Lord."

This is a play with a purpose ; and although —the its incidents are in Russia, it was written by an Conscienc of the Jew Americanised Jew, and is acted by American- ised Jews, for the instruction, correction and reproof of Jews becoming Americanised. It is significant, therefore, that in this, as in the other Jewish writings to which I have referred, it is assumed that in America immigrant Jews get wealth and create wealth. In fact, Jews are the largest productive force in New York and the greatest contributors to its wealth ; and although many of them remain in poverty, and in some parts of the

Ghetto there is greater overcrowding than
in any part of the Pale or, indeed, of the
world, yet in America Jews nowhere crowd
the workhouse nor are they ever a serious
drain on private charity. Those who amass
great fortunes are comparatively few ; but the
average of material well-being is higher than
that which Jews have reached elsewhere.
But if to all everywhere, then especially to
Jews in America, there is danger not only
in the possession, but also in the pursuit, of
wealth. The Jew must work on Saturday
and so violate his Sabbath and disregard
the services of his synagogue if he is to
achieve success. Thus he begins by sins
of commission and omission, doing what he
believes he ought not, and leaving undone
what he believes he ought, to do. "Oh,
if you knew," says a character in *The
Children of the Ghetto*, "if you knew how
young lives are cramped and shipwrecked
at the start by this one curse of the Sabbath!"
Many of the elder Jews, especially those
from Russia, where the letter of the law is
strictly observed, when this discovery comes,
make an heroic sacrifice. Prejudice and
proscription, depriving them of the attractions
of public life in Russia, have thrown them
within themselves to find happiness in their

idealised hopes; and rather than make gain
by denying their faith, they leave the factory
or shop in which they have found employment
and spend their lives as pedlars in order that
they may be free to keep the feasts and fasts,
the holy days and holidays appointed by the
Law. But their children, almost without exception, but seldom from conviction, easily
surrender; and soon they learn to despise
the ideals as well as the practices which they
had been taught to cherish in the Russian
Pale.

A very learned and sagacious Scotsman, Redinteg-
the late Thomas Davidson, who founded in ration
London the Fabian Society, which he left Disinteg-
when it was captured by Socialists, and who ration?
wielded remarkable influence in the New
York Ghetto in the later years of his life,
had the insight and courage to direct a number
of young Jews to the study of Goethe's *Faust*.
He did not say, but in all his teaching of young
Jews he showed that he knew, that the story
of Gretchen is that of many daughters of
Israel in New York—that their nature is funda-
mentally good, like hers, and would suffice
to save them in their old world but is insufficient for the new world of experience to
which they have come—that like her, they are
naïve where they ought to be wise, childish

where they ought to be experienced, romantic
where they ought to be moral, dependent upon
outside ritual and opinion where they ought
to be self-poised. And all this, as Dr.
Davidson implied, is in their case as in
hers, the result of the mediæval training
which prevailed in Germany in Goethe's days
and prevails in Russian Jewry to this day,
in the synagogue, the family and the society
of the Pale. Against the temptations which
beset them in their new environment, the
frail external buttresses of their moral life
are powerless, and before they win any
internal support the sad experience of
Gretchen's life too often becomes theirs;
and we can only hope that in their hearts,
as in hers, God sits in the form of a right will,
and that therefore ultimately, through their
very disintegration, they will redintegrate
themselves. And may we not also hope
for the ultimate redintegration of Judaism in
America, where representatives of all the
countries and customs of the dispersion are
gathered together? Will not a new Judaism
emerge, full of promise both for the Jew
and for humanity at large, when the breadth
and practicality of the German Reformed Jews,
the idealism and spirituality of the Russian
Orthodox Jews, and the simple dignity and

intelligent regard for the past of the Portuguese Sephardic Jews shall have fused with each other and blended all that is best in Gentile culture with the sublimities of the ancient faith ?

But meanwhile the Jewish parent whose son, *The transition Period—* having abandoned Orthodoxy, can never say *Kaddish* over his parents' grave, and whose daughter even has become *Pasha Yisroila*, a sinner in Israel, sees only that the glory has departed from his home and his race ; and the discovery makes a necropolis of his heart. On the night of the Jewish Passover feast, I was a guest in a Boston Jewish home. I had come from Russia, and therefore if I could not repay hospitality with *chiddush*—some new thought on religious topics or some ingenious explanation of a Biblical or talmudic difficulty —as was done in olden days, I could at least give my hosts some news of their own people in their native land. In Russia I have witnessed many touching and inspiring religious rites in Jewish homes. Through the celebration of these during many generations, the sanctity of the home and an idealised conception of family life has become an elevating tradition ; and I have seen a poor Jew, the object of the derision of the Gentiles outside, throw off his garb of shame in the home and

clothe himself with majesty and authority as
he prepared to perform the religious rites of
his race. But on the Passover occasion to
which I have referred, while the parents with
great reverence celebrated the deliverance from
Egypt by solemn observance of the prescribed
rites, the son, when called upon to take the
masta, unleavened bread, and pace up and
down the room with it in symbolic allusion to
the escape from Pharaoh's bondage, and again,
midway in the service, to creep outside the
room and then return to typify the entrance of
Elijah as the harbinger of the Messiah—flatly
refused; and he was upheld by the other
children who openly derided the whole ritual
and the memories and hopes which it was
intended to keep alive. The parents were
heartbroken over their children's apostasy; and
they had also the mortification of knowing that
their parental authority, once supreme, had
vanished.

—and its voes.

In Russia, to this day, Jewish parents, often
through the good offices of the *shadchan*, the
match-maker, marry their children at an early
age and maintain them, it may be during many
years, till they can support themselves, cheer-
fully bearing the burden because, by early
marriages, the chastity of their sons and
daughters may be secured. But in America,

the children support their parents who are
often pathetically dependent upon them, even
as interpreters of the speech and customs of
the people amongst whom they have chosen
to dwell ; and as, in the altered circumstances,
early marriages are the height of imprudence
in those who wish to succeed, the parents see
another of the safeguards of the morality, and
often see also the morality, of their children
swept away.   Nor is another religion or a
higher morality easily or often found.   For
although, outwardly, the Jewish immigrants,
and especially the younger generation of them,
come quickly to resemble the Americans
amongst whom they live, they remain very
unlike them in their inner life, in those deeper
things which spontaneously express themselves.
Thus they are prevented from intimate relations
with the best Americans, and are apt to come
into closest contact with the residual heathenism
of the new civilisation into which they have
come ; and often it is this which makes the
most vital impression upon them during their
first years here, taking hold of the innermost
sources of their lives and colouring their beliefs
and their acts through a hundred hidden veins.
Small wonder is it that the elders, many of
them, "curse their day"!   The Jewish youths,
indeed, seem to be content ; but under even

their heedlessness there still broods silently the
deep religious and moral instinct of the real
Hebrew heart.   In the democracy, are adequate
efforts being made to meet the needs of these
Jews who have lost their guiding star of the
past and are seeking a new ideal in the great
night that has fallen upon their souls?   Or are
native Americans heedless, or even unaware,
of the aliens' need?   And is their own great
need, a man of prophetic insight and poetic
gifts who should come to them

"Singing songs unbidden,
 Till the world is wrought
 To sympathy with hopes and fears it heeded not"?

CHAPTER VI.

RACIAL PREJUDICES.

"So grow the strifes and lusts which make earth's war,
  So grieve poor cheated hearts and flow salt tears;
So wax the passions, envies, angers, hates;
  So years chase blood-stained years
With wild red feet."—EDWIN ARNOLD.

A vast Prejudice—Inevitable Retort—Effects—A Test of
Democracy—The Negro—A new Feud—The first Clash—
No Afro-Americans—Exceeding the Chinese Wall—An
international Problem.

IT has been shrewdly remarked that English- A common
men and Americans have in common a Characteristic.
passion to set the world right and, in attempting this, to concentrate upon other people rather
than themselves, trusting meanwhile that God
will help those who forcibly help some one else.
As an Englishman, I am aware that Americans
have at hand a *tu quoque* to hurl at my head in
reply to the criticisms which I am about to
offer; but, in specialising upon American shortcomings, I am encouraged by the reflection
that I thereby give evidence of a characteristic
which is American no less than English and

79

which my association with Americans has perhaps tended to emphasise. I will, therefore, preface my strictures with the words of a sturdy American colonist, Nathanael Ward, who wrote to King George: "I am resolved to display my unfurled soul in your very face and to storm you with volleys of loyalty and love."

Jews—

Inevitably, when new moral sanctions are being sought, there is danger that some of the fundamental and permanent foundations of morality will be ignored; and when I consider how deep and universal is the upheaval in which immigrants in general, and Jews in particular, are involved by their transference to America, the remarkable fact to me who have seen much, and heard more, of their demoralisation, is that these foundations have been so little disturbed. I recollect Jews whom I have met in America—men like Secretary Straus, Judge Mack and Rabbi Felix Adler, prominent in politics, education and philanthropy, who have settled the ancient quarrel between the life of thought and the life of action by leading both—and many others unknown to fame with whom I have lived in social settlements and in their homes, whose lives are noble and serviceable from end to end; and as I consider that the Jewish race has proved itself the greatest historic influence to affect beneficially every aspect of modern civilisation, I realise that some Jews are already of the forces that are maintaining American national ideals, and I grow confident that, were all who are pouring into the country properly related to the best American life, it would be with the co-operation, if not even under the leadership, of Jews that America would marshal herself for a new intellectual and moral advance. But, unfortunately, the great mass of Americans say, with placid contentment, that, as the immigrant has been given the rights of American citizenship, all their obligation towards him has been fulfilled ; and so they abandon him to the worst influences of his new environment, and too often his citizenship becomes a menace to the State.

Nowhere is citizenship a harder problem than in the America of to-day ; and nowhere is citizenship more heedlessly conferred. The cosmopolitan population, diverse in language, race and religion, and divided and subdivided in industrial occupations and interests, has created the finest, the most intricate and the most delicate of all worlds, in which failure as a citizen involves greater disaster than in any narrower and simpler world, while success demands a more sensitive moral judgment, a more creative imagination and a deeper sense

—given much, but not enough.

6

of the meaning and dignity of life. Yet so
far from any adequate attempt being made
either to keep immigrants out of the country,
or, when they have been let in, to fashion
them into capable citizens, they are freely
admitted and then are sharply shut off
by racial prejudices from the opportunity
of their amplest personal development. Of
their presence Americans say, as the witty
Frenchman said of Catholicism in his own
country : "We can neither do with nor without it."

The
inevitable
Effect.
This prejudice asserts itself against the Jews.
Certainly, it is not as intense as that against
which in earlier times the Jew has stood, and
in other countries in our own day the Jew still
stands, helpless and dismayed. No more has
he to endure great personal disrespect and
mockery ; no more is he subjected to positive
ridicule and humiliation. Yet prejudice against
him exists and must be accepted as a fact,
deplorable in its extent and fraught with
incalculable danger. And even in America,
Jews, not excepting the most successful, many
of whom I have closely scrutinised, fail to shake
themselves entirely free from the traces of
self-questioning, self-disparagement and lower-
ing of ideals which ever accompany repression
and are bred in men who live in an atmosphere

of contempt however carefully the contempt
may be veiled.

Evidence of a vast prejudice abounds on Anti-Semit-ism—
every hand. It finds expression in the term
"Sheeny," which is American for Jew.
"Do you think that I would go and hear
a Sheeny talk?" an American, whom I had
not supposed to be illiberal, asked me, not
without scorn, when I had suggested that
he should come with me to a Reformed
synagogue to hear a famous Rabbi preach.
"The house is full to overflowing," I over-
heard an hotel clerk say to an applicant for
a room who, like myself, had neglected to
make arrangements in advance of arrival.
But when those who were behind, and of
whom I was one, were preparing to go elsewhere, we were told that there was accommodation for us all. At the cost of a lie the
clerk, acting under orders, had protected us
from contact with a Jew. And the Jew,
doubtless, merely pretended to be deceived,
and without any pretence was embittered,
by the *ruse*.

One of the most charming women in the —all in-clusive—
country whose women are supposed to
excel in charm, proved to be a Jewess. Her
features did not bewray her, and for a time
she found no necessity to declare her race;

but when at last, under an obligation of honour, she made it known, she was treated as a pariah by many of those who had been her most trusted friends. A professor at a college upon which he sheds lustre, with whom I once discussed the racial problem, has a daughter who came home in tears complaining that her companions had charged her with having crucified their Lord; it then dawned upon the sensitive soul of the child that, although alike in heart and life and longing to her playmates, she was shut out forever from their world by a veil which even her father, for all his fame, could neither tear down nor creep through. Of course, isolated instances such as these may be found in every land where Jews are found; but in America, more clearly than in any other country that I know except Russia, they are symptoms of a disease that threatens the life of the nation. I met an old fellow-student who holds an important academic position in America. He finds that there, as never in England, he has to keep strict guard over himself to prevent himself from being vulgarised by anti-Semitic feeling, even although the Jews of his acquaintance impress him as being worthy of esteem. While I was his guest, it

happened that a Jew bought a house in the
street in which we were. Great was the
indignation and loud were the protests of
the other householders, although all of them
confessed that they knew nothing against
the man except his race. In many cities,
as, for example, St. Louis, Missouri, property
in the best residential districts cannot be
acquired by a Jew, and any other who buys
must come under legal obligation not to
sell or lease "to boarding-house keepers or
Jews."

Everywhere that men are there is a natural —a Blot
clustering of social grades. In this there is on Democracy.
not necessarily any violation of democratic
equality, just as there is none in giving to
each man a coat that fits instead of giving
to all men coats of one size. But where
social groupings and social ostracisms are
determined by race distinctions, and racial
prejudices exclude men from society for
which they are personally fit, the great
democratic principles—liberty, fraternity and
equality — are all denied, and especially
fraternity which is the test and touchstone
of democratic power and progress. To give
universal liberty is to afford every man the
highest possible scope for the play and
development of his personality. Equality

also means exactly that ; and racial prejudice, which is itself the denial of fraternity, denies to all who are prejudged exactly that liberty and that equality. American democracy, weighed in the balances which immigrants provide, is found wanting. As voters, aliens are of interest to the unprincipled politicians who tend to deform them. When, as men, they claim access to those by whom they might be transformed, they are repulsed. They ask for bread and are given a stone. And votes are as dangerous weapons in the hands of men to whom full opportunity of becoming enlightened, honest and patriotic has been denied, as stones were in a sling which a Jew called David used with deadly effect.

'he Negro
'roblem—
Against all alien groups, and not against Jews alone, prejudice exists ; and negroes are the largest alien class, although the term is seldom held to include them. The negro problem is a race problem. Here I refer to it simply in its relation to immigration, which is our present theme. Owing to new economic forces which are at work, there is a new demand for labourers in the South ; and in all the States, from Virginia to Texas, an earnest and systematic effort is being made to induce them to come. One of the

members of the Committee on Immigration recently appointed by Congress is reported to have expressed the fear that a large influx of European immigrants to the South would occasion "a clash" between them and the negroes. There is as great danger from the migration of labourers from the Northern to the Southern States. Northerners have always claimed to be dominated by higher ethical principles than Southerners in reference to the negro. But fundamental race antipathy exists in the North; and if it is not accompanied by friction, that is simply because there is little social and political contact of the two races. When, and in proportion as, such contact comes, the Northerner, who has not the Southerner's comprehension of the negroes, shows himself less tolerant of their faults and more hostile to their claims than ever the Southerner was. The negro problem is ever shifting its phases; and now that industrial prosperity is attracting the working classes of the Northern States and immigrants from abroad to the Southern States, the race feud in the South is slowly becoming one between the Northerners who fought to free the slave, on the one side, against the negro whom with shedding of blood they freed, on the other side; and the Northerners now have alien immigrants and the negroes have their old Southern masters as their respective allies.

—a new 'hase. This new feud is only at its commencement; but it threatens to be as bitter as ever the old struggle was, even in the dark reconstruction days that immediately succeeded the Civil War. The first "clash" was heard by all the world in the Atlanta riots. Commenting upon these, the author of *The Autobiography of a Southerner* says: "There is a dark and unfathomable abyss of race feeling. While I write, my hope recedes and the pathos of my country deepens. This is the most serious and threatening problem with which the American nation is faced." He traces the riots to the machinations of unprincipled politicians. But he is on the wrong scent unless indeed, as is possible, he means by politicians the labour leaders. The new industrialism, reinforced by the old race hatred, was the cause. Atlanta has become an industrial centre of some importance and has attracted numbers of those whom the negroes call "po' white trash," whose bitterness gave the riot its intensity and scope. There were, indeed, rapes, real and fictitious, to be avenged. But when Southern men take revenge for such offences, they hunt down

the individual who has committed the crime
and, when possible, bring him before the
victim to get evidence of guilt before applying
lynch law.   At Atlanta, however, there was
undiscerning fury against a race.   The new
alignment to which I have referred is already
in process.   A committee of Southern negroes
and Southern white men has been formed for
the protection of the negro race.   Booker T.
Washington pronounces the formation of this
committee the most important step ever taken
by Southern white men for the solution of
the race problem.   But it is merely a new
phase of the old problem.   It is the defence
of the negro by the Southern white man of
the old slave-holding class which the negro
traditionally respects, against the "po' white
trash" from the North and from abroad.

This struggle is not restricted to the Southern
States.   In the North, side by side with a
general altruistic sentiment, there is a quiet
but growing movement adverse to the social
and economic advancement of the negro; and
when Northerners group together in the South
and form a majority of the population of any
town, their prejudice asserts itself in measures
more inimical to the negroes than Southerners
ever adopted, as, for example, at Mena, Arkan-
sas, where at least two-thirds of the residents

Spontaneous Affinities and enforced Associations.

are Northerners, and where, in consequence, no negroes are allowed to reside or even to pass a night. In the Middle States, there is a stricter social ostracism of the negro and an active and open opposition to his industrial and political ascendancy; and recently, when negroes were being imported as labourers to the State of Illinois, the labour unions took action, and the Governor of the State threatened that, if the migration continued, the negroes would be encountered at the frontier of the State with Gatling guns. More recent events in that State have served to illustrate still more vividly the violent racial antipathy that exists. And it has to be borne in mind that in America there is no differentiation of the offspring of mixed parentage from that of parents who are both of pure negro blood. I found "Eurasians" in India and "coloured" people in South Africa, separate from "natives" in church and school and in social life, and asserting superiority to them. But I have found no Afro-Americans, only American negroes. All who are connected by blood, however remotely, with the negroes, and however white they may be of skin and temperament and thought, are forced to rank with the African race. Amongst them are many scholarly and cultured men, some of whom, such as Professor Du Bois, have studied with distinction in American and German universities. All their affinities are with the whites who are no whiter than they, yet all their associations must be with blacks. These men, with grim determination, some of them not without bitterness, are educating and train- ing the race into which they have been thrust for the struggle with the race that has thrust them forth.

Immigration from Oriental countries has A World- attracted attention by reason of events at San Problem. Francisco. There, East and West have come into touch with each other ; the scouts have already exchanged shots, and the world's greatest conflict is hourly growing more imminent. It is claimed that the economic demands of Japanese and Chinese immigrants are so few that they threaten the economic standard of living for the working classes of the community. The argument has special force in a country that has a high protective tariff. If the wage-earner cannot import cheap goods, the capitalist should not be free to import cheap labour from abroad. Protection should be for the equal benefit of all classes. But the demands of the labour unions are reinforced by race prejudice, which has found expression in the indignities and insults that have been heaped upon immigrants from China and Japan; and the *Outlook*, one of the least sensational of all American journals, says that an attempt is being made to build along the Pacific a wall of racial prejudice, more enduring than the famous Chinese Wall, to prevent all free commercial and intellectual intercourse between this Western nation and those nations of the East. In San Francisco I found a "Japanese - Korean Exclusion League"; and at Seattle I learned that this league had sent its representative, Mr. A. E. Fowler, to organise branches there and in other parts of the State of Washington. In *Collier's Magazine*, I find a description of this man: "A labour agitator—Japanese his specialty. He has a compelling kind of crude eloquence and his one idea is—hatred of the Oriental." This race hatred burns fiercely along the whole, Pacific Coast. It reaches to Canada and is not less intense in British than in American breasts. Immigration is more than an American problem. It is a world problem. As such, its effective regulation is only to be found in international treaties. It is probable that, after the Committee upon Immigration has submitted its report to Congress, the American President will call an international conference to consider the whole subject. Italy proposed such a plan informally some years ago, and Greece and Sweden are known to be ready to join the Powers in some agreement that will check the emigration of their citizens. America, as the country which receives the most immigrants, would have the best right to be heard at such a conference; but, unfortunately, America does not know her own mind. There are Restrictionist, Selectionist and Exclusionist camps; and, perhaps, in the multitude of counsellors wisdom will be found. But there are no Expulsionists; and it is certain that the millions of immigrants already in America are here to remain. The immediate need, therefore, is that these should be Americanised. Fortunately for America, social settlements and other agencies are, without prejudice, addressing themselves to this task.

CHAPTER VII.

SOCIAL SETTLEMENTS.

"May I reach
That purest heaven, be to other souls
The cup of strength in some great agony."
GEORGE ELIOT.

Outer Service—Inner Relationship—"Unsettlements"?—Charge
of Irreligion—Jewish Sabbath and Christian Sunday—Hull
House and South End House—"America's one Saint"—
Reformers in a hurry—Influence of "Head Workers."

Compen-
sation.

I HAVE described the social injustice that
is inflicted upon large classes of "aliens"
by the racial prejudices with which large classes
of "natives" are afflicted. It is Meredith, is
it not, who says that the compensation of injustice is that in that dark ordeal we gather
the worthiest around us? In American social
settlements, the worthiest citizens are rendering
to immigrants and others the service which we
have seen to be required—bringing them under
the play of the higher influences of American
civilisation; uniting the scattered industrial,
social, racial and religious elements that are

94

thrown together to make up the community and the nation; giving to all equal opportunity for the development of each personality; and enabling them to hold family life together while they become part of the new national life into which they have come.

This is a national service which is rendered The Plan by the men and women who, in settlements, and Scope— identify themselves with the life and interests of these and other classes of the community, and by individual and organised effort guide them into channels in which the prevailing influence is the common good. Their achievements range from personal influence upon individual lives to collective influence upon national legislation, and the instinct of self-preservation should suffice to awaken national interest in them and their work. Many of the immigrants come from countries in which the Government has destroyed, in its subjects, all respect for objective law. Where no law is fixed, none can be sacred; and many aliens, up to the moment that they embarked for America, have known no other law than the arbitrary will and the changing sentiments of officials in the Russian Pale. The settlements, many of which have arranged their plan and scope with special reference to immigrants, and are practically institutions for the Americanisation of the foreigner, take these restless and lawless spirits on their arrival on American soil and teach them that in a democracy liberty and law go together, that the rights of citizenship imply duties, and that government is of the people, by the people, for the people. The Educational Alliance to which I have already referred, and which is rightly included in the list of settlements issued by the College Settlements Association, every Friday at a patriotic demonstration gathers 800 or 1000 children who have recently arrived from Russia and pledges them to allegiance to the American flag in the following comprehensive formula :—

"Flag of our Great Republic, inspirer in battle, guardian of our homes, whose stars and stripes stand for Bravery, Purity, Truth, and Union, we salute thee! We, the natives of distant lands who find rest under thy folds, do pledge our hearts, our lives, our sacred honour to love and protect thee, our Country, and the Liberty of the American people forever!" By bringing such influences to bear upon the imperfectly assimilated mass of the population, settlements have done much to give a legitimate direction to the great social forces of democracy and cosmopolitanism which else had been even more disturbing as a factor in the life of the nation than we have seen them to be ; and in proportion as the nation perceives the greatness and glory of this result, the task will evoke still deeper enthusiasm and elicit a more adequate response.

To estimate settlement work, one must know individual settlement workers and corporate settlement life. Always, it is out of the central absolute self-core that a man's real influence comes; and especially in the case of a community of educated men and women who have made a breach with their own environment and established their home amongst people whom they seek by neighbourliness to help to social, intellectual and moral betterment, a large part of any good that may be accomplished must simply irradiate in ways hidden to their self-consciousness, without deeds, without words of counsel or teaching, simply through the atmosphere of a higher order of life. Next in importance to the personal character of each worker is the adjustment of all the workers to each other and to their work in the settlement in which they reside; for the influence on the people outside its walls can be no better or more real than the relation of the residents under its own roof. Settlements have been compared to the mediæval monasteries; and it holds of these, as it held of those, that the standard of outer service can

—and the Life and Work, of Settlements.

7

be no higher than the tone of the inner relationship. What any settlement has to contribute to the neighbourhood is determined by what it is in, and has for, itself.

A Jewish—   The charge is frequently brought against settlement workers that they are not religious and that they eliminate all religious elements from their work. "I call the settlements unsettlements,"—a young and Orthodox Jew—a *rara avis*—said to me, attempting a *jeu de mots*, "because they unsettle the religious faith of my race." His contention, as I understood it, is not without force. Immigrants in general, and Jews in particular, have a passion for being quickly Americanised. They are attracted to settlements by the means to that end which they provide. Their ambition is to be genuine American citizens, and the settlement resident is, in their eyes, the representative citizen. When, therefore, they whose whole religion has been ritual find no religious exercises of any kind in the settlement, they infer that the resident has no religion. Religion, therefore, is not necessary to American citizenship—*quod erat demonstrandum*. This argument was confided to me when I was living in the University Settlement in New York. The district in which this settlement is established is almost entirely Hebrew. Of the thousands whom I met in the institution, there was not one, excepting some of the workers, who was not a Jew. On neither the Christian Sunday nor the Jewish Sabbath was there any sort of sacred service. The ordinary Sunday programme is as follows :— 10 a.m., meetings of four clubs and an athletic association ; 2.30 p.m., meeting of the Central Federated Labour Union ; 3 p.m., a children's entertainment and meetings of four clubs and a choral society ; and at 8 p.m., a popular concert and meetings of six clubs. On the Jews' Sabbath, which commences on Friday evening, there are meetings of literary, dramatic and whist clubs, and dancing classes. At Hull House, Chicago, when I was there, a new venture of a "Five-cent Theatre," in which "living pictures," not of sacred incidents, were shown, was started on a Sunday evening, and attracted Italians, Greeks, and Jews.[1] The settlements, I know, are between Scylla and Charybdis. Christian services would savour of proselytism and offend those for whom the settlement exists ; and Jewish services would suggest apostasy and offend the Christians by whom the settlement is maintained. But it would seem that a middle course is not steered by making Sunday and Sabbath days of un-

[1] See Appendix III.

interrupted entertainment.   Nor does the fact
that Jewish settlements devote the Sabbath
to religious services for old and young, and
for "Orthodox" and "Reformed" Jews, make
the danger less.   The simultaneous entertainments, say the elder Jews, keep the young
from the observance of their own sacred rites ;
and the omission of sacred rites in the Christian
settlements, which are regarded as distinctively
American, is accepted by the Jewish youth as
proof that the observance of religious ceremonies
is merely a sign of being still un-Americanised.

−and a
ientile−

In a Chicago newspaper I came across a
reference to an attack that had been made,
in a Christian denominational magazine, upon
Hull House Settlement as an irreligious institution "still surrounded by an undiminished
tide of vice and degradation," and as being
in unpleasant contrast with a mission station
which "in a similar neighbourhood had revolu-
tionised the condition of things."   I know
nothing of the mission station referred to ; but
certainly Hull House has not rid its district of
vice and degradation.   One of the most vicious
places of entertainment which I came across in
America I found practically cheek by jowl with
this settlement.   But Hull House is not, and
has different aims and methods from, a mission
station.   It has wisely resisted the temptation

to lay stress upon what Miss Jane Addams has
called geographical salvation. Its endeavour
has been to make its neighbourhood realise
that it belongs to the City as a whole, and can
improve only as the City improves ; and it has
not been unsuccessful in its endeavour to create
a consciousness of solidarity.   —Charge
                                                   against
The charge of irreligion is, however, serious. Settle-
I am old-fashioned enough to believe that ments—
without a religious motive no life can rise to
great heights of self-abnegation, far less achieve

"The most difficult of tasks, to keep
    Heights which the soul is competent to gain,"

and that no community which is not welded
together by a religious faith can find the glow
and inspiration necessary for sustained altruistic
effort. Religious features, as they are ordinarily understood, are indeed conspicuous by
their absence at Hull House, as elsewhere.
Social settlements, in which I do not include
churches which have absorbed some of the
methods of these, are a particular sign of a
general attempt that is being made in America,
and not in America alone, to restore souls to
order and righteousness by enlightening vice
and lawlessness. This, in turn, is a token of
a superficial notion of evil which forgets or
ignores the natural instinct of perversity which

is contained in the human heart; and, owing
to this fundamental error, many fanciful
extravagances are mingled with great generosity in religious, educational and legislative,
as well as in social work.   In America in
general, and particularly in New England,
which at first was Calvinistic, many are seeking
to correct an undiscriminating narrowness by
an equally undiscriminating breadth.   The
great positives of the Puritan theology have
been abandoned before the greater positives
of any new theology have been won; and
undoubtedly many settlements, having "sup-
pressed sin" (to adopt Renan's phrase), do, in
their work, refuse its remedy—doubting its
poison, they merely film over its wound.   And,
to be perfectly frank, I have met residents in
settlements of whom, as of the fly in the amber,
one wonders "how the devil it got there"—
men and women who had lost their vision of
God and of the spiritual world; who had no
sense of mission or of message; who had not
even an adequate sense of the significance and
value of life.   But I have met in churches
also, those who lack the vision which is alone
granted to high thought and noble purpose;
and in settlements they are relatively few.   I
have tried to discover their motives.   Ordinarily, they have not been accurately analysed

by themselves. Some simply seek the activity natural to every young and healthy intellect, and find in work amongst the poor an outlet for superfluous energy and a satisfaction of intellectual craving such as the ordinarily congenial American task of money-making could not afford. A few are merely incumbents of university fellowships founded for behoof of sociological students—mere statisticians who regard the poor simply as specimens to be analysed and tabulated—mere creatures who would "peep and botanise upon their mother's grave."

Most, however, are young men and women —refuted. of generous instincts, who, in college, have learned to apply to their conduct a social test —a lesson which is being so well learned that the long-standing reproach against Americans that their cultured and leisured classes do not devote themselves to the public good will certainly some day be wiped out. These are good Samaritans, whom to repulse were to show the irreligion with which they are charged. Those who love and serve their fellow-men, and seem to be cold towards God, are more religious than those who seem to love and serve God and are cold towards their fellow-men. The Church, claiming to renew all things through Christ, cannot be Christian and be hostile to those who strive, however imperfectly, to wrest the direction of social progress from the enemies of Christ. And, indeed, only those whose minds have been cramped into believing that their conceptions of truth and service have exhausted all the possibilities of the Eternal Spirit could fail to find in the Social Settlement a revival, as a real force for the guidance of human life, of the doctrine of the divine image in man and the divine life of service of man taught by Jesus Christ. Living in American settlements, I have found myself in an atmosphere of ideality and fellowship which exerts its pressure upon all, giving the uplift of a common purpose to men and women of various races, religions and predilections and of differing antecedents and outlook on life, who exhibit, not the neutrality of indifference, but the tolerance of those who deeply believe. Who could fasten irreligion upon Miss Jane Addams, of Hull House?—who has written :—

"The Hebrew prophet made three requirements of those who would join the great forward-moving procession led by Jehovah. To love mercy and at the same time to do justly is the difficult task ; and it may be that these two can never be attained save as we fulfil still the third requirement, to walk

humbly with God, which may mean to walk
for many dreary miles beside the lowliest
of His creatures, not even in the peace of
mind which the company of the humble
is popularly supposed to offer, but rather
with the pangs and throes to which the poor
human understanding is subjected whenever it
attempts to comprehend the meaning of life."

Or, upon Mr. Robert A. Woods, the head
worker of the South End House, Boston?—
who has written :—

" Professor James has suggested that the
religious feeling at its best seems to depend upon
some sort of fresh ethical discovery.   There is
a certain recognised spiritual light that lies over
all the many different sorts of human effort
that make up the present-day historical movement toward a higher social system and a nobler
type of personality."

I have quoted from these two because the Founders
character of a settlement and of its work of Settlements—
depends upon its head workers, and the foremost
of these are these two.   England has Florence
Nightingale ; America has Jane Addams who
is easily the foremost woman in America.
Mr. John Burns, I believe, called Miss Addams
America's one saint.   Hers is, indeed, a
devout, benignant, valiant womanhood.   She
has a woman's full share of sensibilities and

sympathies, yet she is accurate, circumspect, and symmetrical. She is of a meek and quiet spirit, yet she has the self-possession of the woman of culture and experience. To say that a woman, and that this woman, is one of the greatest influences affecting American life is the highest praise that can be spoken of it and of her. Mr. Robert A. Woods is not as popularly known as Miss Addams, but he has been, and is, one of the formative forces acting upon settlements. He is a man of clear insight, sensitive imagination, comprehensive mental grasp and fertility of ideas; and he also, although his mind is moved by energies that rush into it from the heart, has intellectual and moral poise.

—and Their Influence.

These qualities which characterise the leaders of American social settlements have proved invaluable to their cause. Men prone to "impetuous eagerness, hectic mental spasms, and the appetency for change" went into settlements before these had gained public confidence. The newspapers gave great prominence, for example, to Mr. Stokes as a settlement resident. He is a man materially wealthy, by repute a millionaire, but not mentally affluent, who yielded to the propensity which some persons have to renounce their accidental advantages; proclaimed himself a Socialist;

took up his abode in the University Settlement of New York ; and married a Russian Jewess, a cigarette-maker, I understand, whom he met there. Here was a man anxious, doubtless, to be genuine and to do good, but impatient of slow methods and easily deluded by his own hopes, and easily led into extravagance by a sensibility which domineered over all his faculties ; and he with others like himself sought to rush forward social reform irrationally and emotionally and in disregard of established economic principles. But, being met with firmness and discretion, he and they have publicly avowed their disbelief in settlements and so established public confidence in them.

CHAPTER VIII.

SOCIAL SETTLEMENTS (*continued*).

"Bear ye one another's burdens."—ST. PAUL.

Movement towards Federation—A new Profession—Settlement Workers and the Universities—Moral Value of Education —English and American Settlements compared — The relationship of Equals in a Democracy.

A new Profession. AMERICAN settlements are cautiously, moving towards a national federated union. Already in New York, Boston, Chicago and other large cities there are local federations; and an effort is being made, under competent direction, to co-ordinate the work of all, so that while each settlement retains its own essential qualities, and concentrates upon its own district and its own special problems, the combined intelligence and motive of a comprehensive and organised body may be brought to bear upon the larger questions of social reform—the common general problems of all settlements. Even now, settlement workers in their own localities

are a compact phalanx of conscientious, up-
right men and women, friends of the public
good, who are sanely seeking the amelioration
of the common lot.   The great majority of
them are only of average faculty and have no
great elevation or breadth or profundity of
mind ; but, by living a broadly human life,
they inspire confidence and trust, and by
organised effort under wise leadership, they
exert an influence that is sometimes powerful
and is always salutary upon public sentiment,
municipal action, and State and national
legislation in regard to some of the most
pressing problems of American life.   They
do not, indeed, take direct part as largely as
their English *confrères* in municipal work as
representatives of the districts in which they
have chosen to live.   This, I think, is a
grave reproach ; for there is no greater need
in America than that an end should be put
to the exclusion, self-imposed, of the more
cultured classes from their proportionate
share of authority and responsibility in the
governing machinery of local and national
politics.

Notwithstanding, settlement residents in
America are perhaps more influential in
public affairs than the residents in English
settlements.   Not only are they better

organised; they have a larger opportunity
in America, where the public service is no
professional, and there is, therefore, much
less jealousy of outside interference than in
England, and much more readiness on the
part of local authorities to accept the advice
and assistance of settlement workers.   The
head of a Federal Department has more than
once requested a settlement to transform into
readable matter a mass of material, which
had been carefully collected into tables and
statistics, for the good of tenement - house
people who sadly needed this information
Besides, probation officers connected with
the Juvenile Court often reside in settlements
and render help to the Judges in many ways
Adjoining Hull House, really a part of it, is
a complete boys' club-house in charge of
Mr. Joseph Riddell, who is, or was, probation officer to the district—a house built
by a benevolent lady who, as president of the
Juvenile Court Committee, raised money to
pay probation officers until they were provided for by law.   It is, indeed, settlement
workers who are becoming "professional."   I
have said that a social sentiment is growing
in America which leads men of independent
resources to devote themselves to the interests
of the community; but the number of such

men is still small, and the proportion of
salaried workers is higher than in English
settlements.   In a pamphlet addressed specially to students, and entitled *Social Work,
a New Profession*, the Warden of South End
House, Boston, says, with American directness
of speech, that means are provided which
on an average are on a par with those of
the clerical and educational professions.   This
method works well in America.   That the
labourer is worthy of his hire, is a doctrine
that commends itself to the American mind;
and the labourer is made to prove its truth
by his works.   This secures efficiency; and
in, and in connection with, colleges and
universities, courses of study are provided
for students who are preparing themselves
for this new profession.   In Boston, the
school is conducted directly by Simmons
College and Harvard University; in Chicago,
the institution is part of the University; and
in New York, there is a complete affiliation
with Columbia University through which
students of the school enjoy all the privileges
of students of the University, although the
school is conducted by the Charity Organisation Society, in order that it may be kept in
closest possible relation to practical work.
I have met many college graduates who are

in these schools taking a post-graduate year in professional training which will count towards higher degrees; and I have known school - teachers, physicians and clergymen who were in attendance at them in order to gain a first-hand acquaintance with social needs and to be in a position to judge rationally of proposed social remedies. There is a beginning in England of such courses of social training on the initiative of Miss Helen Gladstone and Mr. C. S. Loch; but America leads.

A new social Force.

It seemed to me, on my first acquaintance with settlements in America, that excessive time and energy were devoted to theatrical and other entertainments, and especially to dancing : in one settlement I attended a dance every night of one week, including Sunday, and some of the permanent residents were not less heroic. Now, I should bear the affliction with greater resignation than I did then; for I have discovered that local conditions impose the abundant provision of amusements upon the settlement if it is to fulfil its mission. The corrupt political leaders have hitherto directed and controlled a large proportion of the social agencies in their communities, in order that they might more easily manipulate the social forces of their particular wards. The settle-

ments in such districts render no mean service
by devoting equal initiative and enterprise in
making themselves a social force that asserts
moral standards. Any dancing that I endured
was with Jewesses from Russia. As a rule
they were very well dressed—adorned, not
decorated. Some of them looked better clad
than fed, as if they practised the precept of the
Rabbinical proverb, "Put the costly *on* thee
and the cheap *in* thee," or had paid heed to the
advice of the famous translator of Maimonides,
who wrote to his son, "Withhold from thy
belly and put on thy back." Beauty is, indeed,
of ethical importance, even mere beauty of
raiment, as those Jewish teachers understood;
and at the settlement entertainments, the
desire of youth to appear finer and better and
altogether more lovely than it really is gets its
proper direction and, when necessary, its proper
curb. I asked every Jewish maiden who was
partner of mine whether she had ever danced
before coming to America. Few, if any, of
them had. The *besyeda* of the Russian village
is not found in the villages of the Jewish
Pale where the conventions forbid the
dance. But in the new conditions the old
conventions are soon flung aside; and there
are few young Jews of either sex who do not
learn to "trip the light fantastic toe," and to

8

speak of dancing in this Miltonic phrase, almost as soon as they set foot on American soil. The Ghetto has few public-houses, but innumerable "dancing saloons"; and it is undoubtedly a safeguard which young men and women win when, at settlement dances, they form new conventions which impose restraints upon themselves and upon those whom they meet in their own social life.

New Methods.

Education is undertaken in American, as in English, settlements. It is the weakness of this work in both countries that academic methods are too exclusively employed, so that only a few of the people of the neighbourhood who happen to be of the academic type of mind are reached and influenced. This was to be expected owing to the fact that the residents are, for the most part, college men who are imbued with academic ideas which it is most difficult for them to modify. But more completely than in England, although still incompletely, settlements in America are shaking themselves free from the methods employed in schools and colleges and are adapting education to the special needs of the working people of their districts. Speaking generally, I should say that American settlements have more flexibility, a power of quicker adaptation, larger hospitality of mind to new ideas, greater readi-

ness for experiment, and greater ease in changing methods as environment may demand, than
the English settlements have hitherto shown.
So, in America, amongst the Jews who are a
music-loving race, a music school settlement
has been established; and people interested in
it send tickets for the best musical events, so
that the pupils are able to hear the finest inter-
pretations of the great musical compositions.
I found a large nurses' settlement which, in
addition to the ordinary organised social and
educational features of the settlement, has a
large band of trained nurses distributed
throughout the city, and has besides, as a
unique feature in educational work, an apart-
ment which serves as a schoolroom for classes
in domestic sciences, where a systematic course
is taken in the care of the home. Each pupil
must master, for example, the cleaning of the
stove, and the building of the fire, before
being promoted to the more advanced course
on cooking. In one settlement, I sat down
to a meal which had been prepared and set
by neighbourhood children who waited upon
their teachers and me. These girls may not
go into domestic service; but such training
will prove useful to them in their parents' home
and when they take up homes of their own;
and I learned that many girls of the neighbour-

hood apply for special instruction of this kind
before marriage.

This social method of teaching has often
far-reaching results. A series of " gay little
Sunday morning breakfasts " was given in the
Hull House Nursery to a group of Italian
women who were wont to bring their unde-
veloped children to the settlement for hygienic
treatment. At these social gatherings the
mothers were educated to the recognition of
"the superiority of oatmeal over tea-soaked
bread as a nutritious diet for children "; and
as, under the influence of baths and cod-liver
oil, the children grew straight and strong,
there disappeared from the children's necks
certain bags of salt originally hung there
to keep off the evil eye which had been supposed to give the children crooked legs and to
cause them finally to waste away—disappeared
also from the parents' minds an old superstition
which, by academic methods, would never have
been overcome.

In America, more completely, I think, than
in England, settlement residents become part
of the common life of the neighbourhood, share
in the joys and sorrows, the occupations and
amusements, of the people, and associate with
them on equal terms, without patronage on the
one side or subserviency on the other. The

relationship is accepted as that of equals, in a manner and with a completeness which, in a less democratic country, neither party to it would allow. In England, where class distinctions are undoubtedly more clearly defined, social workers are tacitly admitted, by those in whose interests they work, to be of a superior class and are treated as men and women who have come down voluntarily from a higher sphere to minister. The "neighbours," by their looks and words and bearing, confess inferiority and dependence; and so they unconsciously offer a subtle form of flattery which gives "philanthropy" a fictitious charm. In America there is no trace of this; and settlement residents are winnowed by the relationship of equals which obtains and which is much more difficult to sustain than that of superior to inferior. In consequence, if there is less culture, there is perhaps more character in American than in English settlements; and, if there are fewer residents who are men of independent resources, there are, it may be, more resourceful men.

There are more than 200 social settlements A new in America. In them, the best minds and Hope. hearts of the nation are found, fully alive to the need of breaking down all barriers that separate the different races of a common land.

Therein is ground for hope. The rays that give to the valleys light and warmth, first gilded the topmost peaks alone; and, by an inevitable law, the entire community, within reasonable time, will be permeated by the spirit that now animates only the noblest citizens. The influence of settlements to this end is not less important than that of the Churches: many of these, indeed, retreat before the flowing tide of immigration, sell their consecrated buildings for conversion into synagogues, and salve their consciences with the reflection that the poor have the settlements always with them. And, possibly, immigrants who have fled from the persecutions of Christian rulers, will be more disposed to accept the Christian faith, when they shall have partaken of such of its fruits as settlements provide.

CHAPTER IX.

EDUCATION.

"Why, if the Soul can fling the Dust aside
And naked on the Air of Heaven ride,
    Wer't not a Shame—wer't not a Shame for him
In this clay carcase crippled to abide?"—OMAR KHAYYÁM.

Idealism of first Settlers—Its permanent Influence—Seen in
    educational System—Progress in Education—Education
    and Speech—The Language of America and England—
    The Future of English—Education as Discipline, and as
    democratic Training—English and American Methods
    and Results—Dangerous Tendencies.

IN nothing can the traces of colonial American The edu-
influence be more clearly seen than in the cational
educational system of the modern American System—
Republic. It was not until after the Revolution
that it was generally recognised that education
in all its phases and grades must be encouraged
and made universal under a democracy in which
the rights of opportunity were to be equal ; and
it was only during the nineteenth century that
the present great system of schools completely
covered the land.   Yet, as early as 1649 every
New England colony except Rhode Island had

made public instruction compulsory, and required that, in each community of 50 householders, there should be a school for reading and writing, and in each town of 150 householders a grammar school with teachers competent to fit youths for the university. The Virginian settlers did not show equal enthusiasm for education; and for about three centuries there were few schools in Virginia, which, indeed, was long without any towns of 150 householders, or even of 50, the Southern settlers having tended to dispersion and isolation on large tracts of land, unlike the New England settlers, who gathered in groups of families, forming villages and towns. Now, however, a common school system, with modifications to suit local conditions, prevails in all the States of the Union, from the Atlantic to the Pacific, and from Mexico to British America; and, although the Southern States still lag behind, they are rapidly moving towards equality in this respect with the other States to which they have always been superior in other and not unimportant respects. There is in the schools great inequality of equipment, instruction and organisation; but everywhere there is manifest a movement towards uniformity of improved methods of instruction, and public schools are rapidly coming to be

related together in a system of schools, flexible
and adaptable to American manner of living,
American social ideals and American national
ambitions.

In the wide sweep of this educational system, —is be-
some angles and eddies are still missed. There coming universal
are illiterates in every State. A considerable in Scope.
proportion of the negroes and "mean whites"
of the Southern States can neither read nor
write, and many of the adult immigrants never
learn so much as the English speech. By
reason of the high average intelligence in
America, the ignorance of these classes seems
denser and is more dangerous than that of
analogous classes in other countries. An
illiterate class in the midst of an educated
community presents such a complete state of
discord that the effect is out of all proportion
to its cause; and many of the worst evils of
American municipal and political life spring
from the remnant of American citizens whom
the national system of education has left un-
touched. As poverty in the midst of wealth
is aggravated, so ignorance in the midst of
intelligence is intensified, by the contrast; and
the evil of illiteracy forces itself so constantly
upon public attention that, by evening adult
classes for immigrants, special schools for
negroes, and laws making attendance at ele-

mentary schools compulsory between the ages
of 8 and 14, strenuous and not unsuccessful
efforts are being put forth to make education
universal in its scope.   Nearly one-fifth of the
whole nation of 80,000,000 people is constantly
at school; and one in every 160 Americans is
a teacher.   Many of the teachers, it is true,
lack a broad background of knowledge, especially those in the rural schools which enrol half
of the entire number of school children; and
when a teacher teaches right up to the edge of
his knowledge, and the pupils detect in him
a constant fear of falling into the abyss, the
teacher necessarily lacks the sense of assured
power which alone can make his words com-
pulsive and fructifying, and the pupils feel most
impressively the influence of what the teacher
is careful not to say.   But the equipment of
the teacher is improving every year, and
secondary and collegiate education are making
such rapid strides that, while between 1876
and 1904 the population of the United States
increased only one and three-quarter times,
the attendance at high schools and colleges
increased thirty-fold.   In an evening school
for immigrants I saw written on a blackboard:
"If the torch of liberty is to enlighten the
world, it must be fed from the lamp of knowledge"; and Americans are so persuaded that

this is truth, and the whole truth, that they are apt to ascribe too much rather than too little power to education as a civilising force, forgetful that the sources of human action lie deeper than the brain.

Much that relates to the common schools of a country can be learned from the common speech which, indeed, reveals so much that it is, perhaps, no exaggeration to say that the soul of a people, the quality of their deepest life, the secret of their spiritual state, is discovered by the new meanings that old words have gained, and the old meanings that they have lost, and even in the modifications in pronunciation of them that have taken place. Therefore, while I cannot pretend that in America I spoke little, I certainly was careful to listen much, in mindfulness that, as rare Ben Jonson said, language most shows a man. *Its Influence seen in—*

I do not profess to speak with any authority upon the vexed question of the relative merits or demerits of the speech of the two great nations which have English as their mother-tongue. To be in a position to judge impartially and adequately, it would be necessary to have been born and educated in both countries, and to have mingled freely with all classes of society in every English county and in every *—the vulgar Speech.*

American State. This initial impossibility
accounts, in great measure, for the grave and
often ludicrous errors into which all have fallen,
even those learned in philological science, who
have attempted the task. What hope, then,
is there for an unlearned Scot who was at
school in England and has spent many years
furth of all lands in which English is the
common tongue, hearing and perforce speaking
other languages than his own? Yet, to one
poor negative qualification, I may dare to lay
claim. By virtue of long residence abroad,
my ear has not become dull to the peculiarities
in speech of either, and quick only to those of
the other, country. When, in an American
school, a child is uncorrected for saying "he
done it," my ear is certainly offended; but not
more than when, in an English school, there
is no challenge of "he had got," in which no
less than in the American phrase, preterite and
past participle are confused. And if, in common
with most Englishmen, I foolishly resent the
American constant use of the word "sick" in
the sense of Shakespeare and the liturgy of
the English Church, I resent equally, and with
equal folly, in common with all Americans, the
English occasional use of the word "stink" in
the direct fashion of the Gospel according to
St. John. This is my infirmity; and I have

learned in suffering what, in these paragraphs,
I seek to express in prose.

In neither England nor America is the ^{The} mother-tongue as well spoken as in either ^{English Lan-} Germany or France. The *minutiæ* of the com- ^{guage—} plicated grammar of their respective languages is and must be carefully drilled into French and German children in the schools; and between those who have, and those who lack, the mastery of these languages, speech makes a gulf which is necessarily greater and more fixed than that which separates educated from uneducated among a people whose language, like the English, has few grammatical changes. Absolute accuracy of speech is rare, in both England and America, by reason of the very ease with which relative correctness may be gained in the English tongue; and to English and Americans alike, in the matter of speech, as in many other matters, one has constantly to say : " Who art thou that despisest thy brother?"

Many Americans have assiduously taught me, ^{—a liv-} in correct English phrasing, the nice shades of ^{ing Organ ism—} meaning of American slang which, as it appeared to me, is different from, more expressive and not more vulgar than, English slang; and such of it as is unstained by vulgarity or unweakened by foolish extravagance of idea or phrase, although, unfortunately, not such alone, is gradually making a place for itself in the speech of Americans and Englishmen, to the enlargement if not the enrichment of our common language. Against the evils of this process, the increase and diffusion of education is the only defence. The court of final appeal upon language, in every country, is all the speaking-people of the country; and they, by their own usage, enforce their own decrees which may be modified, but are never wholly determined, by the presumptive authority vested in precedent or in the rules and standards which purists provide in a conscious effort towards the logical precision and symmetrical completeness which no language has ever attained. Language is a living organism; and as the specific experience of those by whom it is used grows larger and more complex, it responds to meet the exigencies of this expansion, yielding new terms, or new shades of meaning to old terms; and, therefore, only by common education, giving fineness of feeling, and an instinct of consideration, for the instrument of common communion, can its perpetual increase in strength and beauty be ensured. This is especially true of America. For there, the tendency is stronger than in England to consider the speech of any man, as any man himself, as

good as any other; and this application of a
principle that is deemed democratic is pushed
to an extreme by those, and they are many,
who forget that in speech, as in art and morals
and everything that man undertakes, the
freedom and originality are spurious which
cannot move along other than novel paths
and which refuse to obey those simple outward laws which have been sanctioned by the
authority of the foremost men and the experience of mankind.

Yet, as the level of popular education in
America is, at least, not lower—I rank it higher
—than in England, I was not surprised to find
the average speech in America not less accurate
or refined than in England, when I compared
it, not with the speech of the cultured section
of English society, which is the misleading
comparison that is ordinarily made, but with
the average speech in England—the only just
comparison. The American voice differs from,
and to the undoubted advantage of, the English
in inflection and pitch. In pronunciation,
however, the American seemed to me to excel
in distinctness and the Englishman in distinction; and this, perhaps, is what was meant
by W. D. Howells when, in a reference to
Harvard, he spoke of the "beauty of utterance
which, above any other beauty, discriminates

—has differenti- ated in America—

between us and the English," and by Professor
Jowett who said that in his lecture room at
Oxford, he had seen pass before him "several
generations of inarticulate-speaking Englishmen." The superior distinctness of the
American is due, I suppose, to conscious
efforts, as the superior distinction of the
Englishman is due to habitual and uncon-
scious ease, in conforming, each in his measure,
to the standard which educated persons in both
countries, even in America, accept.

—but not
leterior-
ited.   Strenuous, and not unsuccessful, efforts are
made in American day schools and night
schools to counteract the pernicious effects
of foreign influence upon the English speech.
The number of new foreign words or phrases
grafted on to the language is remarkably small
relatively to the number of foreign immigrants,
whose influence is greatest upon pronunciation,
especially of complex consonantal sounds ; and
such alterations in speech as result from the
fusion of the heterogeneous elements of the
American population is not a deterioration
of the language. The original substratum
of Anglo-Saxon in our common language
was overlaid with multitudes of conversational
words from the French, of literary and ecclesiastical words from the Latin, and of technical
words from the Greek, long before there was

any America to have any speech; yet the mixture of Normandised - Gallicised - Latin with a base of Anglo-Saxon gave us "Chaucer's well of English undefiled." And although now, the robust American people, especially in the Western States, too often seem to think that in order to be vigorous, they must be vulgar, in their speech, and there is to be found in all the States, on the one hand, a passion for coining new and unnecessary words and, on the other hand, a tendency to banish from use a number of the most useful and classical expressions by the poverty-stricken device of making one do duty for a host of others of somewhat similar meaning, yet, as successfully as in England, the corrosive and debasing influences that always act upon the substance and texture of a language are being resisted in America; and the vitality and freshness of Americans' speech, springing from the fulness of American life, is ample compensation for the anæmic refinement of speech in which Englishmen are apt to take pride. And every increase of popular education in America is a new guarantee of the security there of the English tongue.

In other directions, the influence of the American educational system is powerful and far-reaching. In no proper sense can children *The educational System has disciplinary—*

9

be said to desire education ; but "the system"
has come to be regarded by practically all the
children in America as a vague, mysterious
force, irresponsible and irrevocable, over which
they have no control.   It is as one of the
processes of nature to them.   They cannot
accommodate it to their whims.   Violations
of its requirements, like violations of the laws
of health, bring their own certain penalties.
The tasks which it imposes cannot be shirked,
transferred or postponed.   This is valuable
discipline, and it is almost the only discipline
which multitudes of American children receive.
For, while American family life has a pervasive
quality of tender devotion and considerate
courtesy unexcelled in any land and the moral
standards retain much of the potency of their
puritanic origin, the puritanic severity has
entirely disappeared from the family discipline ; and in nearly every home in which I
have been, whether of the rich or the poor,
the children were the masters of the house,
believing as a principle that everything turns
upon them, and seeing, in any rare order that
might come to limit their encroachments, an
abuse of power, an arbitrary act.   The children
are the test of the domestic system, and that
system in America *laisse à désirer*.   And I
failed to understand how the children grew

into law-abiding citizens until I left the home and went into the school. There I found them, by a rule which is impersonal and in- variable—as domestic rule should be—learning obedience, order, integrity in work, steadfast- ness in spite of moods and submission to the rightful demand upon each individual of the entire community in order to the harmonious action of all. Thus, by a discipline that is ethical and is maintained during the formative years, the children acquire the social and civic habits, and are formed for liberty—not the false liberty allowed in the home, which, if unchecked in the school, would breed lawless- ness and chaos, but the liberty of work, of service and of growth.

The spirit of democracy, which is essential —and de- in the great Republic, is maintained by many mocrat- of the institutions of the country, and especially Effect. by the public schools. There are, as I have said, many private schools for such families as prefer their exclusive ways : it is estimated that the number of children attending these is one-twelfth of the number in public schools, and that, I understand, is about the proportion which is to be found in England. But the significant fact is that there is a steady decrease in the number of private schools and in the number of pupils attending those that survive.

Private high schools for a time showed greater
vitality than private elementary schools; but
even in these there has been a decrease of no
less than 1500 since 1902, in spite of an increasing population. The sceptre has passed
from the private schools; and in the common
schools, not only rich and poor but also natives
and immigrants meet together on a footing of
strict equality, taking their places according to
what they are and not what they are called,
each, under its undiscriminating rule, finding
his natural level wholly regardless of the conventional circumstances of life. In America,
freedom was gained only by sacrifice: the first
settlers won it by exile; the founders of the
Republic bought it a second time with shedding
of blood. Liberty, thus had and held, became
their passion, and thus America has been saved
from the danger to which other democracies
have succumbed in preferring equality so far
above freedom that they were willing to be
in servitude if only they had equality in it.
Equality they always had—the first colonists
started as equals. What was so easily gained
was not so highly prized; and Americans have
never taken as jealous and constant care to
preserve equality as to maintain freedom. But
by the public schools, as one of their inci-
dental but most important influences upon the

national life, equality has at least been so far retained that it is more nearly realised in America than in any other modern State.

I have never had the advantage of being in the teaching profession; but I have long understood that in America, more than in England or any other country, text-book instruction predominates over oral instruction. In the schools which I visited, I found that harm to the pupils from the method of throwing them upon the printed page and holding them responsible for its mastery was averted by most of the teachers. These, by a process of question and answer, sometimes most informally carried out, forced the pupils to assume a critical attitude towards the statements of the book, to test and verify them or else disprove them by appeal to other authorities or by actual experiments. Text-book memorising, if it is not being supplanted, is at least supplemented by the method of critical investigation. In the very lowest classes great attention is paid to answering questions in complete sentences, arranging thoughts in the child's own language, and describing objects exhibited to the class. Arithmetic, which receives more attention than in any other country, probably on account of its commercial value, is generally mental arithmetic. Written work is rarely called for,

Its characteristic Methods.

and slovenliness characterises such of it as
there is; but always the pupil is prevented
from being a mere recipient, and is called on
to think, to observe, to form his own judgments,
even at the risk of error and crudity. So the
mind reacts for itself on what it receives, and
education is made to unfold the learner as well
as the facts. This is very different from the
English methods which tend to deify correctness and exactness in written exercises and to
repress individuality of thought; and here we
come upon the secret of some differences
between the American and English peoples.
Englishmen are methodical and accurate;
Americans are ready and alert. Englishmen
write better than they speak; Americans speak
better than they write. A writer who com-
bines broad information with the power of
clear and convincing expression is rarer in
America than in England. In American
newspapers and books, there is a great blaze
of talent but a lack of distinction of style—the
accent of good company is wanting; English
literature has metaphors, it has music, it has
colour, but, compared with American literature,
it lacks soul and life. Some explanation of these
differences is found in the common schools.
Both countries must educate their masters and
teach those of each to unite the methods of both.

We have seen that in the primary and secondary schools education is free and that the principle of free education has been carried further by the establishment of free training schools for teachers, and, in some States, of free universities. The principle has been pushed further still; and in the primary and secondary schools, text-books and stationery are provided at the public expense. It may be that the just demands of the citizen upon the State have not, in these measures, been exceeded. But there are ominous signs of the growth in America of what Burke called a valetudinary habit of making the extreme medicine of the State its daily bread. In many quarters, I have heard the demand that school children should be supplied with food and clothing at the expense of the State ; already, in the States of Colorado, Indiana and Vermont, clothing is furnished by taxation, to enable children to attend school. During my first visit to New York, a movement was on foot, in responsible quarters, to provide skilled oculists to treat all pupils in the schools who have defective eyesight, and to give eye-glasses to all for whom they are prescribed, the entire expense to be borne by the State, regardless of the ability of all or some of the parents to meet the cost involved. This was urged as a natural develop-

Its doubtful Tendencies.

ment of the work which has been done in providing free books and stationery; and, although the representatives of the Charity Organisation Society and other philanthropic societies laboriously pointed out that this new proposal was not a logical outcome of the old practice, the distinctions which they drew seemed to the general mind distinctions without a difference, and, as if in recognition of this fact, emphasis was put elesewhere than on principle in the opposition to the proposed extension of the " free system "—*e.g.*, upon the inability of the Board of Education to raise sufficient funds for other and more necessary work. Eternal vigilance will be required to prevent the growth in America of paternalism of the most complete and demoralising kind. The combined evils of trusts and municipal corruption which are being eradicated are less disastrous than this evil will prove if it is allowed to take root; for it would affect every individual in the nation and breed manikins where, if anywhere, men of unimpaired independence, individuality and force are required. As it is, there are many who fear that by "electives," "co-education," the great preponderance of women teachers and the lack of religious teaching in the schools and colleges, the educational system is threatening the virility of the nation.

CHAPTER X.

CO-EDUCATION.

"For woman is not undevelopt man
But diverse."—TENNYSON.

"The Teacher's Face"—Teachers' Attractions and Distractions
—Their freedom from sordid Aims—The preponderance of
Women—Its Effects—Advantages of Co-education—Some
serious Defects—A Chicago Experiment—A national negative Failing.

THE educational process is not the Teachers'
mechanical impact of text-book or meagre
Salaries—
even of idea upon the intellect, but the
impact between living beings; and in the
interaction of these, vastly more is given and
received than is ever formulated. What the
teacher is, expresses itself; and always the
teacher's personality is the greatest educational influence. It is, therefore, necessary
to know American teachers in order to appreciate American education. It was inevitable
that, during a year amongst Americans, I
should meet some of the 500,000 teachers
who are in the United States. Not only did

I not seek to avoid, I courted, my fate, in spite of a paragraph which I had read in the *Educational Review* : " We all know the teacher's face ; it is worn, sacrificial, anxious, powerless." Doubtless, there are American teachers to whom those words would apply ; but I have rarely met them. The Jewish face I have often seen. And not infrequently, I have seen at the scholar's bench and the teacher's desk a face which gave a hint, mysterious and elusive, of all ages and all nations ; and I have wondered whether that is the type that will be and will prevail in this land to which,"from all the ends of the earth, all races have come to be the ingredients of the ethnic stew".

A meagre salary may cause a meagre face ; and neither in school nor in college will a teacher's ordinary income carry him much above want. Americans spend vast sums of money upon every part of their schools' equipment, except the human which alone is indispensable. Teachers are legion, and therefore the aggregate amount paid to them is imposing ; but the average salary is small and inadequate. It cannot be said that teachers take no thought for income ; in Los Angeles, I heard much of a Miss Margaret Haley, of Chicago, who has sought to organise teachers into a union which should federate with labour unions for

common ends. The good sense of the great
majority of representative educators and educa-
tionists assembled in convention at Los Angeles
led them to repudiate this movement as de-
rogatory to themselves and their profession,
and antagonistic to the principles of public
education at public expense; and all over
the country hosts of men and women are
following the profession of teaching with a
devotion that takes no undue account of
pecuniary reward. The great attraction for
them is that they find special facilities for the
use of powers which they rejoice to use; and
I have found teachers the most attractive class
in the nation, because more than any other
class, not excepting the clergy, they are free
from sordid aims.

Each State "raises" its own teachers; but —but
in summer, at vacation schools for teachers, at abundant Life.
Chautauquas, and at educational conventions,
teachers from all States meet and mingle in
the closest fellowship. Those whose work
lies in small towns and country districts
ordinarily select a great city of a distant
State for their summer resort in order that,
while pursuing studies which shall enable them
on their return to their schools to use themselves to the top notch of their value, they
may also enjoy a complete change from their

ordinary conditions and cultivate interests
unconnected with their official tasks.   This
policy is pursued every year by a large proportion of American teachers, in spite of
their meagre salaries; and I had the privilege
of giving letters of introduction to five of
them who had arranged to spend their
"Sabbatical year" on the Continent of
Europe, two in Germany, two in France and
one in Russia, studying educational and economic conditions in those countries.   Doubtless,
some merely get familiarity with names that,
at some sacrifice of sincerity, does duty for
knowledge; but the majority are honest in
their desire and effort to learn more and
be better able to teach, and undoubtedly
these do at least contrive to maintain such
freedom from exhaustion and such mental
hospitality as are valuable assets in a teacher
and can only be had by uniting some disinterested pursuit with professional work.   In
America, more completely perhaps than in
England, teachers keep the roots of their
being fed by the cultivation of their individual
tastes in books, amusement and travel; and
powerlessness, according to my observation,
is peculiarly absent from the teacher's face.
It should also be said that, by the intermingling
of the teachers of the several States, there

is being fostered a sense of fraternity in effort, achievement and destiny; and thus a vital relation between the schools in all parts of the vast continent is being established and is already having a beneficial influence upon the educational interests of each part, especially in raising the standard of education in those parts where hitherto it has been lower than the average which prevails. In consequence, there is an approach towards uniformity in the educational standards of the different States, although there is not even the semblance of national control.

Meeting American teachers was not made less attractive by the fact that it meant meeting American women. In 1870 there were 77,528 men and 122,795 women teaching in the elementary and secondary public schools. Last year the number of men had increased to 109,179; but, as the number of women had risen to 356,884, the preponderance of women teachers is greater to-day than ever before, and there is every indication that it is destined to be greater still. Already, of every group of ten teachers in "cities" with a population of 25,000 and over, eight are women; women number seven of every group of ten teachers in smaller "cities," towns and villages; and throughout the

Women Teachers of adolescent Boys.

whole country, of every four teachers three are women. If any man suddenly addresses any American boy who is under eighteen years of age, he is likely to be styled "M'am" in reply : I tried the experiment many times and gave it up lest I should become confused as to my own sex. Women are the teachers of the American youth. This may be as it should be in elementary schools ; and perhaps American sentiment is right in depreciating a man who is willing to spend his time and strength in the details of the primary school, where a woman's patience, discrimination and sympathy can best understand and train the fickle fancies, moods and impulses of a child. But in the high schools, boys of eighteen years of age whose physical nature needs the most careful development are taught by women who sometimes are not many years their seniors ; and men have told me that they now recognise that serious injury was wrought upon them at that period of their school life when, lonely, shy and sullen, they were left to fight through their crisis, not knowing that it was a crisis that came to all and was necessary in the development of life. I met few serious teachers of either sex who did not deplore the excessive preponderance of women on the teaching staffs of secondary schools and the higher classes of elementary schools.

These facts must be considered in connection Mixed with the system of co-education—*i.e.*, the Classes and the education of boys and girls in the same classes moral Problem. —which is the general practice, not only in the primary schools, but also in the secondary which, it must be remembered, pupils ordinarily enter at fourteen, to remain until they are eighteen years old. Richter said that, to ensure modesty, he would advise the education of the sexes together, but that he would not guarantee anything in a school where girls, still less where boys, were alone together. He would be a bold man who should guarantee anything in any conditions ; but the consensus of opinion amongst American teachers, than whom none have a better right to be heard, is that sexual perversion and sexual tension are appreciably diminished by the co-educational system of American schools. So far as this claim can be established, the system must receive the sympathetic consideration of all who realise the gravity of the moral problem of our schools.

But other results, less obvious and far from The excellent, are forcing themselves upon the deepest and most attention of American teachers. The deepest permanen Effect. and most permanent effect of co-education is upon adolescent boys. A girl reaches and

passes the period of adolescence at an earlier
age than a boy. When, therefore, pupils of
fourteen enter the high school, the girl is from
two to three years more matured than the boy.
In seriousness of purpose, in power of application and in womanly instincts, she is already
a woman ; but the boy is still under the
ferment of mind and body which in him also,
but not until two or three years later, is to
result in nubility. Consequently, in all work
that requires concentration the girl excels ;
and as in most, if not all, high schools the girls
greatly outnumber the boys, the courses of
study, by an inevitable process of evolution,
have become adapted to the special capacities
of the girls. Thus, in classes taught by
women, boys are taught, with girls, studies
that are peculiarly suited to girls, and the boys
do not have from the teacher, who is a woman,
the comprehension of themselves and their
moods that the girls receive. The boys are
in a minority ; and, as the irrepressible
tendency to imitate the majority asserts itself,
they become an inferior copy of girls, winning
a girl's gentleness and sensitiveness but not
the proper strength of either sex. Tried by
a woman's and by a girl's standards, the boys
prove inferior ; and when at last they enter
upon their full heritage they are irreparably

—As re-
cognised
by a
Chicago
teacher.

wounded in their dignity and have lost the faith in themselves of which, in order to play a man's part in life, they have the utmost need. There is no greater danger to character than this.

Impressed by these considerations, a high school principal in Chicago, with the consent of the Education Board of that city, began recently to separate boys and girls during their adolescence, in order " to accustom them in their early teens to differentiate in their characteristics so that they shall be prepared for the higher complementary relations of life." This is surely a wise and necessary step. The same thing may be strength in the woman and weakness in the man, and what is good in the woman may be evil in the man. Below the virtue which is evangelical and sexless, there is a virtue of sex. This deeper virtue the American man must take heed to retain ; for a man, a nation, an epoch become effeminate sinks in the scale of things. The question with regard to America which, more frequently and urgently than any other, has forced itself upon me, relates to the national virility upon which national greatness ultimately depends. I was in New York when an election campaign was afoot ; and I met a typical political " boss " —a man who knew how to mingle truth with lies, to appeal to the generous as well as the baser instincts of men, to overawe as well as cajole, and to assume the air of superiority to self-interested passions while most devoured by selfish greeds. I am aware, and I make large allowance for the fact, that it is a failing of mankind, and not merely of Americans, that evils to which we have become accustomed do not strike us with the horror and dismay which would be wrought in us by a new evil of less degree; and Americans have grown familiar with the political corruption which is the shame of American public life. Yet, it is an attack upon the very foundations on which a democracy rests; and by the manner in which it is met the democracy must be judged.

—in the American Man— From time to time, in New York and elsewhere—for the evil is everywhere—the superior social section, always sensible of the danger and disgrace, works itself up into a flurry and demands legislative and other contrivances to deliver the nation from its peril. But while all are willing to be saved, few are resolved to work out their own salvation, and none, it would seem, glory in the privilege of suffering for that end. If it could be gained without effort, or by one spasmodic effort, or by the continuous effort of some power not themselves that made for righteousness, or if personal effort did not involve personal sacrifice, the better men and women would overcome the corrupt politicians who are numerically an insignificant fraction of the people. But, finding that they cannot do everything easily and at once, they see no alternative but to do nothing at all; and, being unwilling to pay the price of freedom, they cease to assert their right to govern themselves, and submit to government by a gang of unscrupulous men who are organised to limit and restrain the exercise by the democracy of its political powers and who joyfully sully their reputation for an end the very opposite of that of Danton, who exclaimed: "*Que mon nom soit flétri, pourvu que la France soit libre.*" It is not the honesty, it is the moral courage of Americans, the splendid virility of the early settlers, that seems not to have been adequately maintained. The corrupt minority prevails because the majority weakly shrinks from the strain and stress, the toil and turmoil, the opprobrium and slander, and the prolonged endurance of these, which is the price that *must* be paid for the reform which is desired.

In *Les Femmes Savantes* of Molière, Ariste —being lost? says to his brother Chrisale—

> "Your wife, between ourselves,
> Is by your weaknesses your ruler.
> Her power is only founded on your feebleness."

The negative failings of the honest men in America form a basis for the positive wrong-doing of the men who are corrupt; and the penalties of duties neglected are ever to the full as terrible as those of sins committed—more terrible, perhaps, because more palpable and sure.   And, with the best will in the world, I cannot find in American co-education of the sexes by women teachers any promise of adequate correction of the tendency to prefer the hard to the easy course even when the hard happens to be the right course, which is seen, in its consequences, not only in politics but equally, and with equally disastrous effects, in other phases of American life.[1]

[1] See Appendix II.

CHAPTER XI.

SECULAR EDUCATION.

"The soul of politics is the politics of the soul."—ARISTOTLE.

National Virility and the national Schools—An educational Catchword—Church and State—The passing of religious Instruction from the Schools—Moral Values of secular Studies—Sunday Schools—Absence of sectarian Strife—Contrast with England.

I N the last analysis, national virility depends Educa-upon ethical and spiritual vitality; and I tional Fallacies have, therefore, been specially interested to see how far this is nourished in the national schools. Often I have asked teachers what they consider to be the chief necessity in education. More than once the answer has been given in a phrase which seems to be the present educational catchword: "Send the whole child to school." I ventured once to suggest to a group of teachers that, in this phrase, a demand is made which is by law implicitly disallowed. The teachers were quick to see my drift; and, in the course of an interesting discussion upon religious education that ensued, an admirable

149

précis was given of a significant article or
lecture upon that subject by an American
college professor. The restriction of religious
education to the Church, involving the exclusion of it from the schools, was held to imply
three educational fallacies. First, it divides
the historical content of culture into parts and
assumes that these parts can be communicated
separately; secondly, it divides the pupil into
parts and assumes that these parts can be
developed independently of each other; and
thirdly, it divides the teacher into parts and
assumes that certain elements of his own culture
can be kept out of the class-room. Thus, only
a part of the child, a part of the teacher, and
a part of culture is by law admitted into the
schools; and in proportion as this theoretical
denial of the child and the teacher as each an
indivisible unit, and of the vital correlation of
studies, prevails in practice, the American
educational system is a thing of shreds and
patches, the American child is only partially
educated, and the American teacher's personality is incomplete in the school.

Indirect
religious
Influence
of
Teachers.

Some teachers vaunt their limitations and
openly proclaim their belief that religion is not
essential to human life and will gradually disappear. They, and such as they, push the
principle of secular education to an extreme,

and show a narrow and nervous determination to banish from the schools and from school books all reference to Christianity and its positive beliefs. But undeniably their number is small and their influence is not great. Most teachers are themselves religious ; and, in spite of constitutional and statutory prohibitions, they take the whole self to school and bring their entire personality to bear upon those whom they teach. In one way or another, within or beyond the limits imposed upon them, the teachers make education a constructive religious influence. Undoubtedly, it proves such to multitudes of the children who are taught in the public schools ; and this, not direct religious teaching, is the real religious influence on a child, even as the atmosphere, transparent to the direct rays of the sun, receives its heat from the rays given off by the surface of the earth.

Yet here may apply the precept : "This ought ye to do, and not to leave the other undone." Americans maintain that their Republic rests upon a religious idea. But, having disavowed external authority in the State and refused to allow the Christian religion to be taught in the schools, they have never frankly introduced into either the ideal upon which the State is declared to rest. Thus

Moral Values of secular Studies.

both State and school are really without
religious sanctions, except such as are surrep-
titiously introduced from the religion which is
disallowed.

Substitutes
for
Religious
Education.
It was otherwise, perhaps more completely
than was wise, in the earliest days of education.
Then, schools were founded "to baffle that
deluder Sathan" by bringing every pupil to
"a lively faith in Jesus Christ." The State
was to be strengthened by the development of
the character of the citizens, and direct religious
education was the principal means to that end.
*An Spiritus Sancti Operatio in Menti sit
Causa Naturalis impropria Erroris?*—"May
the work of the Holy Spirit in the mind be
the improper cause of natural errors?"—is a
specimen of questions that had to be discussed
by candidates for the degree of Master of Arts
at Harvard University in 1742 ; and so recently
as fifty years ago there were at Williams
College sixteen compulsory religious services,
four noon class prayer-meetings, one college
prayer-meeting, and six other regular but not
prescribed religious exercises every week.
Then, the aim was to make the human will as
a strong house, barred and bolted, that could
withstand every blast of any storm. Now, the
aim is to protect the house, as by a forest on
which the fury of the storm shall be spent.

Æschylus attributed all wrong-doing to
παρακοπά, false coinage, the impress of a false
affectional value on things. American education seeks to distribute the affections, in their
intensity and proportion, according to the true
worth of things ; and the attempt is made, by
education that is not religious, to bring the
motives, which are the forest protecting the
house, into harmonious relations, and produce
that equilibrium of good which is accepted as
the perfection of human conduct. In consequence, one hears, on all sides, of the relative
" moral values " of the secular studies of the
schools ; and there is perceptible, I think, in
every rearrangement of courses of studies an
effort, whose motive does not always rise into
consciousness, to give greater place and
emphasis to those subjects which are supposed
to have the value which was ascribed to
religious teaching in former days. History, it
is said, illustrates ethical principles, and enlists
the dispositions on the side of right ; and history,
therefore, which has been the most neglected
of all the main lines of study, is gaining greater
recognition in the schools. Choice works of
plastic and pictorial art, and other objects of
sense perception, are rapidly finding their way
into the classrooms because of the moral values
which they are held to possess ; and music,

for the same reason, is steadily growing in importance.

The chief Hope. But reliance is chiefly placed in imaginative and dramatic literature ; and I have listened to discourses to teachers upon the moral value of Dante's *Hell and Purgatory* as showing the nature of sin, of his *Paradise* as showing the nature of righteousness, and of Shakespeare's *The Merchant of Venice* as showing— But why trouble to show the moral value of that play ? Do not the Jews insist that, because of its unlovely Jew, it, along with the Bible, shall be excluded from the schools ? And is not the insistence of the Jews likely, sooner or later, to prevail ? The end of all earthly learning, as Sir Philip Sidney says, is virtuous action, and the best educational method is certainly that which "moveth us to do that which earthly learning doth teach." But the majority of teachers, even in America, are not able to perceive, in every subject that they teach, the processes of humanity's effort toward ideal living and to give it definite and direct moral value to a child ; and indeed, the value of literature in forming high ideals of conduct and in inspiring to their realisation will, perhaps, always prove to be in proportion as moralising is eschewed.

It is claimed that the educational system has the day schools as merely one of its parts, the other part being the Sunday schools, and that, as the function of the State is to teach secular subjects, to teach religion is the function of the Church. Whatever educational or other fallacies may underlie this theory, a noble and vigorous effort is being made to give effect to it by bringing the Church to realise and fulfil its responsibilities with reference to that part of national education ascribed to it. Religious teaching, excluded from the day schools, is being systematically and thoroughly promoted in the Sunday schools which in America, although they are still shamefully inferior to the public schools, are greatly superior in their teachers, their methods, their equipment, their curriculum, their grading and their results, to similar institutions in England. The Sunday school has not become, but it is becoming, entitled to rank as part of the educational system of the United States. The State sees that democracy cannot rest upon an ignorant *demos* and, by the secular education of the children, is ensuring general enlightenment and a great increase of material wealth. The Churches see that democracy cannot rest upon an unspiritual *demos* and, by the religious education of the children, are ensuring that the

Functions of Church and State.

wealth of the nation shall not be a mere mass
of things in which a nation's, as a man's, life
"consisteth not." This is one of the most
hopeful features of American life ; for America
is committed, apparently irrevocably, for weal
or for woe, to exclusively secular education
in the public schools.

Is Faith
found ?—
It remains, however, to be seen whether the
Churches will maintain the educational activity
which they have begun. I confess that sometimes I fear that in this, as in the political
sphere there will be preference of the easy to
the hard course when it is found that everything cannot be done easily and at once. For
even that aspect of American life which most
favourably impressed me immediately on my
arrival in America—the toleration and charity
that prevail in the ecclesiastical world—and
which the Bishop of London and many others
have contrasted with conditions that prevail in
England, gives me pause. Assuredly, it is
pleasant to be in a land where there is not
such fierce strife of sects as exists in England
and was not always, in America, unknown.
But what if the present generation of
Americans be not as loyal to truth and to the
spirit of sacrificial service for truth as were
their Puritan forefathers whose convictions
were shaped by a severer creed and whose

characters were disciplined by a more rigorous
social and religious atmosphere in home and
church and school? What if, in religion as in
politics, the American is genial simply because
he is latitudinarian, is liberal only because he is
not intense, and is tolerant of the convictions
of others merely because theirs are not deep
and his are no deeper than theirs? In- *—if lost,
what else*
difference to religion, as well as indifference to *Avails?*
politics, is as disintegrating a social force as
excessive zeal. To have no creed to inscribe
upon a banner is as anti-social as the flaunting
of the banners of competing and conflicting
parties and sects.

I am a man of peace, but not of peace at
any price ; and sometimes I have found myself
wishing that American pruning-hooks were
turned into swords. The dull level of caution
and kindness seen everywhere except in
commerce ; the hard pursuit of material things
and the easy abandonment of facts and rights
by which a people must live or die—these
things have seemed to me the most ominous
spectacle of American life. If ever, in
England, I should find myself tempted to
despondency by reason of the fierceness of
political and ecclesiastical contentions, I shall
put to myself the question which, without
particular reference to England or America,

is asked by M. Tardz in his *Les Lois d'Imitation*: "Which is worse for a society —to be divided into parties and sects fighting over opposing programmes and dogmas, or to be composed of individuals at peace with each other but each striving within himself, a prey to scepticism, irresolution and discouragement?" I quoted these words one day to an American Bishop who had quoted the Bishop of London to me. The surrejoinder was a quotation from St. Paul: "Now abideth faith, hope, charity, these three; but the greatest of these is charity." It is not for me to dispute such points with Bishops; but I ask myself: "What if charity 'abideth,' but not faith and hope?" To apostolical authority I submit— when it applies.

CHAPTER XII.

COLLEGES AND CHARACTER.

"I bless God I have been inured to difficulties."
OLIVER CROMWELL.

Growth of American Colleges—Their educational Efficiency—
Their Ideal—American Graduates at English Colleges—
The elective System—Its Abuse—The fundamental
Idea sound—The Future of Electives—Self-Supporting
Students—Self-Government.

OWING to disreputable institutions, call-ing themselves colleges, which have sold honorary degrees, American academic honours and even American colleges have fallen into disrepute abroad. Bogus colleges, however, are and always were relatively few and they are in process of rapid extinction. The State of New York has prohibited the use of the name of college or university where the requirements of the State Board of Regents are not met. The tendency to similar legislative control is apparent in all the States; and all the reputable institutions welcome such supervision as a means by which their *status* may be certified and they may gain recognition as part of the educational system of their State. In 1897 there were 472 colleges, properly so-called, excluding those for women alone; and the large recent increase in the number of those who enter the institutions of higher education may be seen by the following statistics of four of the State universities which I visited :—

	1885	1904
University of Michigan	524	2,900
University of Wisconsin	313	2,810
University of Minnesota	54	3,700
University of California	197	3,057

In 1904, there was a total attendance of 119,496 undergraduate students in American universities and colleges; and the number of graduate students is increasing every year. Some Englishmen have complacently assumed that, because American students come to English universities, American higher education has nothing of comparative value to offer. They forget that students also come from German universities which are, perhaps, the best organisations in existence for the enlargement of the bounds of knowledge, furnishing opportunity and incentive to the student to learn, from libraries, laboratories and living teachers, the best results of investigation and—in some respects of more importance still—giving to students and instructors golden opportunities for continued and successful research.

The American universities have elements of strength and greatness which the English lack;[1] and I am not disposed to quarrel with a Rhodes scholar who, in making a report to his own college in America, which came when I was there, maintains that, admirable as is the training in classics, philosophy, history and other branches of study which Oxford offers, yet from the sole standpoint of scholarship it was not necessary for him to leave America to find the best. Professor Münsterberg, whom Harvard succeeded in taking over from Germany and who has never hesitated to point out the defects of either American or German institutions, acknowledges that the American degree of Doctor is superior to the average degree in Germany; and at the present time, when Oxford feels discontent with her methods, her forces and her conditions, and a commendable spirit of inquiry regarding the university and college administration pre-

[1] See Appendix I.

II

vails, it is a distinct advantage to her to have
a number of picked American graduates in
her schools.

Colleges
and
Character.
Colleges, however, have as their ideal the
development of moral and social as well as
intellectual qualities; and at present my chief
concern is the influence of collegiate life upon
the character of the students upon whom,
as the future leaders of the nation, the
national destiny in great part depends. Some
one has well said that it is the essence of
indolence to be industriously doing easy and
obvious things while arduous duties go undone; and in this sense I have ventured to
say that the strenuous American, no less if
not more than other men, is apt to be an
indolent man preferring the easy to the
hard, even when the hard happens to be
the right course. I have also suggested that
this tendency does not find adequate cor-
rectives in the secular co-educational
primary and secondary schools. Of the
higher education, it has to be said that it
is possible to graduate in it also without
submitting to the severities and virilities
which are a yoke which it is good for a man
to bear in his youth. More than once I
have been asked by youths of eighteen years,
who were about to pass from high school to

college, to advise them in the "election" of studies which they should pursue. I knew nothing of their individual tastes, predilections, aptitudes, gifts or purposes; and on questioning them with regard to these, I found that my ignorance was equalled by theirs. I as little thought of blaming them as myself for that. I did, indeed, blame one of them who indubitably, from the wide election allowed him, chose a course of study known in college slang as "softs" or "snaps" or "cinches," because the work and the liability of failure in it were least. But I laid greater blame upon the elective system which presupposes that the average youth of eighteen, fresh from school, has defined aptitudes, understands himself, has adequately given shape to his ultimate purpose, and can be depended upon to select with insight, courage and judgment the studies best adapted to himself and to the achievement of his destiny.

Originally, in American colleges, the course The Touch— of instruction was fixed. It was assumed that all men were alike, and that certain studies were necessary to, and necessarily gave, a liberal education; and therefore no deviation from a prescribed course was allowed. The educational disadvantages of such a system, rigidly applied, are obvious; but at least it

supplied wholesome discipline for many youths
by making them take what was to them the
hardest, when they would have preferred the
easiest course. With the vast enlargement of
the field of knowledge, a larger view of culture
and a better knowledge of human nature, considerable modification of the old system was
inevitable ; and the fundamental idea of
electives is sound. But in America, the
election goes too often by fragmentary subjects ; and incentives to a weak and foolish
choice are found in the method of awarding
the degree, not for final proficiency in a
coherent and well-balanced course of study in
which, within reasonable limits, freedom of
election has been allowed, but for a pass in four
subjects in each of four successive years, the
whole number of subjects being in some
colleges as disconnected, even as chaotic, as
the student may please. This crude and un-
scientific system came into being as a hurried
and, therefore, ill-considered accommodation to
the demands of the large and growing number
of undergraduates who go to college to prepare
for a commercial or industrial, as distinguished
from a professional, career. Intellectual purposes do not dominate such students. The
scholarly motive is not primary. They seek,
and it must be admitted that they get,

"the touch of college life" which often gives them considerable charm.

During a long railway journey I once had two fellow-travellers who proved themselves men of some culture if not of high intellectuality, men not of a parish but of the world, vigorous and attractive all-round men whose talk was of the relative merits of certain colleges in athletics, in debate and in study, and who themselves discussed intelligently and reverently Comparative Religion and Röntgen rays. I exchanged cards with them and found that one of them was a manufacturer of boots and shoes and the other a commercial advertiser, whatever that may be. Such pleasant surprises are more frequent in America than in England where, indeed, they are an experience I have yet to find; and such men give new dignity to commercial life and do much to redeem their communities from intellectual poverty and from a social barbarism which has too much afflicted American democracy. And who shall say that, in the complex academic life of a nation, occasion and methods shall not be given for the education which consists of intellectual conditions and associations as well as for that which consists of intellectual forces compelling to hard intellectual toil which, of course, must always be a university's chief end? Yet, undoubtedly, under the system which grants a wide choice between departments and between courses in each department, the students who most need compulsion are conceded undue and mischievous indulgence in their whims and caprices, as they follow the lines of least resistance in the elections which they make. Even Charles Francis Adams has said that, at college, he "browsed about, sampling this, that, and the other." He gave up the classics and got rid of mathematics; and he now devoutly wishes that he had never been allowed a

—and the Discipline of College Life.

choice. Electives will never be disallowed again in American colleges; but already they are being intelligently restricted, and it may reasonably be expected that, before long, all students, and not merely such as choose, will be subjected to the discipline proper to academic life.

Students who earn, in order that they may learn—

The best men, and not infrequently the best students, are found amongst the large class of undergraduates who are "self-supporting"— a term which casts no shadow of slight or reproach. These earn their college expenses, in whole or in part; and they are finely disciplined by their four years' warfare for their four years' course. Some one has said that he first met the self-supporting student on the steps of the college library and found him

reading from a volume of Xenophon which he
held in his right hand, while with his left he
sold socks, suspenders and collar-buttons to
the undergraduates ; and this pleasant inven-
tion does not exaggerate the perseverance of
this class of students in their twofold task
of learning and earning. Undoubtedly, some
are seriously hampered in their studies by their
other work ; but, in most cases, the time spent
in making money is snatched from idleness,
recreation or repose rather than from classes
and preparation for these, and often the addi-
tional work is tutoring, night-school teaching,
laboratory and library assistance, or other
occupations which are aids rather than hin-
drances to strictly academic tasks.

The ingenuity and resourcefulness, the —and who
decision and energy, the endurance and cheer- are disciplined
fulness of these students is worthy of the thereby.
highest esteem ; and equal esteem is, perhaps,
due to the other students for their frank and
generous admiration of those of their fellows
in whom these qualities are developed by their
pecuniary need. I was assured by the professors of more than one college that undergraduates who both learn and earn well, receive
too much rather than too little regard. Always,
when visiting a college, I took care to get into
touch with the self-supporting students ; and,

when far from all colleges, I met them at every turn. At the colleges, I found them in charge of furnaces and lawns, tending homes and gardens, and acting as janitors, bell-ringers and caretakers; at Yale University students told me, with satisfaction, of some of their number who served, on occasions, as pall-bearers at funerals in town; and, when I was travelling, it often happened that students on vacation were my drivers, my waiters and baggage-clerks at hotels, and my engine-drivers, conductors and ticket-collectors on trains. Yet, of them all, I can recollect only three who seemed to lack self-respect. At one college, in the Middle-West, professors and students were justly proud of a Rhodes scholar, at Oxford now, a blacksmith's son, who, arriving without a cent, after a long tramp, in the college town, had passed his first night there on the steps of the town-hall, and had afterwards, during his curriculum, earned his lodging, his food and his fees by any and every kind of work that he could find in college or in town. Some colleges and universities have as many as 90 per cent., while others have no more than 10 per cent., of this class of students; but of the entire body of American undergraduates, the average, on a conservative estimate, of those who are self-

supporting is 45 per cent. Thus, there are
no less than 50,000 students in the country
who are constantly under this kind of discipline ;
and, perhaps, the Scotch universities, which
have an analogous class, are the only other
educational institutions in the world that have
as robust a body of men on their rolls.

Being unfettered by traditions, American Self-
colleges are able to strike out on interesting Govern-
and original lines ; and some collegiate author- ment, as
ities, if the term may, in this connection, be Discipline.
allowed, delegate their authority to the students,
on the assumption that self-discipline is the
best discipline, even for youths. This system
of self-government has gained much ground in
recent years. I found it established, in highly
elaborated form, even in elementary schools.
There, without question, its deepest defects are
disastrous. The authority of age, of knowledge, of position and of function, rarely found,
as I have said, in the home, disappears also
from the school ; the scholars learn to claim
the privileges and liberties of men and also
those of children ; and the intelligence and will,
which the system is intended to strengthen, are
insensibly impaired. This innovation is but a
specimen of a large crop of mushroom experiments which spring up in America. Some of
the fungoid growths are grotesque ; many of

them are beautiful ; nearly all of them are non-
fibrous and experimental. Perhaps, when they
have done their work, the right seed will ger-
minate and true reform grow in the mould
which they have prepared. Self-government
in colleges is still in the experimental stage ;
and it may be that, properly safeguarded, so
that the Faculty shall not shirk its proper
responsibility and the students shall not have
too heavy a burden of responsibility laid upon
them, the system will unite the Faculty and the
students in the common effort to make scholars
and men at the colleges, by training them in
self-direction, self-restraint and self-control.

CHAPTER XIII.

COLLEGE ATHLETICS.

" I like a clamour whenever there is an abuse The fire-bell at midnight disturbs your sleep, but it keeps you from being burned in your bed."—EDMUND BURKE.

Undue Importance of Athletics—Their Degradation—A Market for Athletes—The Extent of the Evil—Russian Tchinovniks and American Managers of College athletic Teams—A faulty Generalisation—American Students undemoralised—Explanation—The Beginning of the End of the Evil.

COLLEGE athletics demand more serious The attention than even college electives. Motive of the According to the sayings of Confucius, the Athlete, philosopher K'iung, whose learning was extensive, took up charioteering in order to remove the reproach that he did nothing to render his name famous. In America, neither the colleges that give, nor the students who receive, extensive learning render their names famous until they "take up," and excel in football, baseball, or some other form of sport and prove their prowess in inter-collegiate contests, by the results of which the relative merits of the colleges are determined from year to year. Professor Simon Newcombe, one of the foremost of living American men of science, in answer to his own question why students of Harvard and Yale join the athletic teams of their universities, replies that for the most part the game is not a pleasure to them, but a severe strain which they undertake in order to command the esteem of their fellows and excite the admiration of the public. If they devoted themselves to purely intellectual improvement, they would have to wait long years before getting into the limelight, while in the athletic team they find themselves there at once.

A mean Act.

Perhaps it would be more correct to say that it is to get their college into the limelight that students join the college teams. I happened to be in residence at one of the best colleges in the Middle-West when its students were victorious in the annual State inter-collegiate contests. Yielding to the generous insistence of the students who were celebrating their victory round a huge bonfire in the college *campus*, I said a few words of congratulation which were sincerely spoken; but it would have been impossible for me to utter them had I then known one half concerning athletics in American colleges that I have since learned. I had my first nibbles at the tree of knowledge, and my

eyes were partially opened, at that very college.
The students, recognising my surprise at their
extreme elation, explained that it was due to
the fact that one of the competing colleges had
meanly enticed their trainer from them by the
offer of a higher salary than their college could
afford to pay.   Later, a professor said to me
that the Faculty and trustees rejoiced with
exceeding joy because the enhanced renown
which, by the victory, the college had gained
would attract many new students who otherwise would have gone wherever, elsewhere,
success had gone.

This spirit of rivalry between the various
colleges is one of the most obvious and most
repugnant features of American academic life, as
compared with Germany whose universities are
superior to those of both England and America,
in this, as in some other important aspects.   All
German universities are parts of one great
governmental system, and are in large measure
considered to be equal ; and it is the ambition
of many students to take each of their six
semesters in a different university, passing freely
from one to the other.   In America, however,
excessive devotion to one seat of learning is
mingled with a hostile and depreciatory spirit
towards all others ; and any student who may
migrate from one college to another has to bear

A demean-
ing
System.

the imputation of disloyalty.   Even graver mis-
demeanours are apt to be imputed to him,
should he have the misfortune—I must use the
terms of the market-place, which alone are
appropriate here—to be good athletic material
which it would pay another college to buy in
order to render its name famous by achieving
superiority in inter-collegiate contests.   At a
meeting of college presidents held recently at
Cornell University, it was stated by one of the
presidents, and contradicted by none, that the
various   league   teams   of   the   colleges   are
" bought and sold in the open market."

This seems to hold true of all the States,
even of Oklahoma which attained the dignity
of Statehood only the other day.   This State
resolved to protect itself against the evils which
attended the growth of the other States.   To
that end, it constructed a Constitution of which
it has been facetiously said that to worship it
would be no sin, since it is unlike anything in
the heavens above, or in the earth beneath, or
in the waters under the earth, and therefore
stands outside the limits of the Biblical injunc-
tion as to idolatry.   But the Constitution which
seeks by its provisions to protect the State
from numberless specific evils such as trusts,
gambling, drunkenness and even drinking, has
omitted to provide against the establishment

within the State of an open market where
league teams may be bought and sold; and I
met a pupil of an Oklahoma High School who,
having proved himself good athletic material,
had received from athletic managers of more
than one college in other States competitive
offers of board, tuition, books, "coach" and
other inducements to aid him in determining
the choice of his college on leaving school.   I
am told that the great private schools even
send agents to the elementary schools to buy
up athletic material with which to build up the
reputation of the school.

Much has been heard of the physical and Extremes
of Mean-
intellectual evils of modern athletics.   In ness meet.
American colleges, as in England outside of
the colleges, the chief evil is moral.   Of
recent years, in order to repress professionalism
in college games, a rule has been adopted by
which no student is held to be eligible for
admission to a college team who does not
declare that he has never in his life received
any compensation, direct or indirect, for the use
of athletic knowledge or skill.   The declaration
is solemnly made; and yet no college team
ever meets another with actual faith in the other's
eligibility.   I recollect being much perplexed in
a club in Russia by the pleasure which a member
found in losing a considerable sum of money

to his opponent, a Government official, in a game of cards. When, however, I heard that the following morning the loser had received from the winner a favourable answer to a petition that he had made haste to present, I recognised that I had seen an official bought and sold in the open market in such a manner as left me without a shred of evidence in proof of the offence. *Les extrêmes se touchent*; and athletic managers of American college teams have been known to make wagers with, and lose them to, students who afterwards have enrolled in the colleges from which the agents came. Who doubts, and yet who can prove, that these athletes were bought? By these and other equally disreputable methods, the rules against professionalism are systematically circumvented; and, of course, athletes who are thus dishonourably secured must "in honour" play to win, even although they play in dishonourable ways. I have heard certain college athlete trainers described as "great" in teaching the art of dexterously maiming an opponent; and a college president has publicly stated that to decieve the umpire, to wrangle over a doubtful decision, to rattle the pitcher (that is to confuse the thrower at baseball), to disconcert the fielder who is trying to bring off a catch, and many other forms of discourtesy and fraud, "are openly practised and unblushingly condoned."

From these particulars it would be easy to make a faulty generalisation regarding American students and American colleges. It is true that no man trained in such devices as those which I have described can be expected to show sensitiveness of conscience in the commercial and political world; and I have heard the prevalent corruption of American public life ascribed to the debased athletics of the colleges. But the college graduate is ordinarily, in commerce and politics, a power that makes for righteousness and few corrupt politicians have had a college career. English institutions are sometimes better than individual Englishmen. In America the individuals are ordinarily better than the institutions : the individual conscience is higher than the public conscience. Mr. W. D. Howells, whom I met in New York, said with reference to a recent visit to England that, had he met Harvard men coming and going in mortar-boards and cropped gowns in the quadrangles and gardens of Oxford, he should not have known them from the Oxford men whom he actually saw : the Harvard men might look sharper, tenser, less fresh and less fair, not so often blue of eye and blond of hair,

The Mass of Students not de- meaned.

12

more mixed and differenced, but they and the Oxford men would be easily recognised as of a common race. The resemblances are not less, and the differences are not greater, in the inner life and character of American and English students. In America, as Baron Pierre de Coubertin perceived and said, the students are "*les vrais Américains, la base de la nation, l'espoir de l'avenir.*"

Their Escape explained. That the demoralised athletics of American colleges have left American students as a body undemoralised, is due to three facts, each of which, however, is itself a misfortune, if not a fault, in academic life. (1) Few students take an active part in athletics. All are interested but few play. The great majority are mere spectators of the game. I was astonished by the numbers of students whom I found, at all colleges, content to sit, day after day, on the "bleachers" and see their fellow-students play ; and they, on the other hand, were astonished by the statements of the American Rhodes scholars at Oxford that, there, so many students take part in college sports that ordinarily none are free to be spectators. More than once I have been asked whether it is the case, as an American has declared, that the average for boating, which in American colleges is one man in seventy, is at Oxford one in seven, and

whether the average Oxford college of 150 *An American at Oxford* quoted.
men maintains two football teams, an eight and
two torpids, a cricket eleven, and a hockey
eleven and has, besides, the men who play golf,
lawn tennis, court tennis, rackets and fives, and
the men who swim, box, wrestle and shoot?

Such statements, made by Americans who
are suspected of having become too much
Anglicised, I have almost persuaded some
American students to believe; but I do not
believe that I have succeeded in convincing
one that there is no organised and systematic
coaching of athletic teams such as is practised
in American colleges where professional trainers
ordinarily receive, for a few weeks' work, more
than the best professors get for a year's
academic service. First, then, few students
play; and of these few, only some are bought
and sold. (2) Of the members of the athletic
teams, few ever achieve other than athletic distinction. Such severe training as the modern
college athlete gets is not shaped in reference
to, and is not a basis for, mental training. It
is not easy to make the transition from
excessive physical activity to intellectual
activity or to reverse the movement. The
two forms of expenditure cannot go on
together, or be added to each other, without
an excessive drain on vital forces. Thus, the

athlete becomes a mere athlete and rarely
gains a position in the commercial, political,
literary or educational world in which he could
make his influence widely felt. The American
Rhodes scholars at Oxford are athletic, but
they are not ordinarily chosen from their
college athletic teams. Thus, the corrupted
men do not greatly corrupt, and the incorrupt
represent worthily American academic life.
(3) Few others than the corrupt few have
any knowledge of the corruption that prevails.
The President of Clark University has said
that one of the great dangers of the play of
American students is that, instead of being a
school of honour, it will be a school of dis-
honour. It is such to those who are bought
and sold; and it would be such to all the
students, were it, as so large a part of students'
activities ought to be, within their ken and
did they yet tolerate and condone the evil.
Recently, some professors and *alumni*, as I
have intended to show by frequent references
to their utterances, have courageously set
themselves to the ungrateful but most
necessary task of exposing the evil; and
that marks the beginning of its end. Such
defects as I have cited, are incident to the
youth and rapid growth of American institutions; and they are being overcome. The

American educational system is, as Browning's poetry was regarded by himself,—

"Certes, incomplete,
Disordered with all Adam in the blood,
But even its very tumours, warts and wens
Still organised by and implying life."

To nothing devised and wrought by men could higher praise be given. English colleges also have "all Adam in the blood"; and it will be well for us if we prove as quick to see, as frank to admit, and as resolute to amend defects as later chapters will show Americans to be.

CHAPTER XIV.

THE COLLEGIATE TASK.

"Act so that the maxim of thy conduct shall be fit to be universal law."—IMMANUEL KANT.

Academic Jewish and other Aliens—Their Influence in dissipating racial Prejudices—Collegiate Task: its fulfilment a national Benefit—The Collegiate Task frustrated by College Fraternities.

TEN days after my arrival in America, I found at one of the best colleges that the most influential professor was a Jew who exerts considerable influence, as author and lecturer, throughout the United States. I thus got my first hint that in America the scholar and teacher are quietly and surely taking the place of the money-lender and financier as representatives of the Jews. The genius of this people, not only for commerce and trade but also for literature, law, medicine, music and the fine arts, is making its Americanised members, as artists, poets, philosophers, barristers and statesmen, an important factor in the highest development of the nation. They are amongst the most capable public-school teachers and college and university professors ; they are prominent as journalists, essayists and pamphleteers ; and the extraordinary musical development of America is largely due to them.   In social settlements, in civic federations, in municipal reform leagues, in city clubs and in citizens' unions—in a word, in all societies whose aim is to purify political and social life—they are active and influential members.   Oscar Straus, the most intellectual and one of the most efficient members of President Roosevelt's Cabinet, is a Jew. Judge Mack, the greatest Juvenile Court Judge, is a Jew.   Jacob Schiff, one of the sanest of American philanthropists, is a Jew. Felix Adler, to whom all sections of cosmopolitan New York turn for eloquent support of pure idealism and high moral standards, is a Jew.   Leroy Beaulieu has said that Israel runs the risk of being the victim of the Jew's enfranchisement and of perishing in his victory. The risk is great, as I have shown.   But in America, many Jews show that it is possible for the Jewish race to maintain and develop intellectual and spiritual qualities even better when enfranchised than when enslaved.   Being a Gentile who has lived much in Russia, in

close contact with the governing classes there,
I was not easily convinced of this fact which,
however, now that I myself am at last enfranchised from prejudices to which I was too
long enslaved, I find no less a pleasure than a
duty to record.

Iis Ser-
vice and
hat of the
Colleges
o the
Nation.
Social antipathy to Jews, I have said, exists
in America, in spite of all the religious tolerance, the civic and political liberty, and the
opportunity for men of all nations, races and
creeds of which, not without reason, Americans
are proud.   This prejudice, with its conse-
quent misunderstanding and alienation, in a
nation which has so many hundreds of
thousands of Jews and is receiving hundreds
of thousands more every year, not only
suggests a war of classes in the future but is
narrowing and blinding to both races now,
making both poorer and meaner and preventing the growth of the relations which
should exist between the common citizens of
any State and most completely in the democratic United States.   The separating barriers,
however, the educated Jews overleap; and
from the other side they begin to break them
down.   This holds true of other immigrant
races; for although not so many of their
members pursue the higher education, there is,
on the other hand, less prejudice against them

to be overcome. The colleges, in thus re-
inforcing the sense of fraternity in civic
destinies through fraternity in learning and
letters, are continuing their earliest mission;
for the claim made on their behalf must be
conceded, that the intellectual was the first
kind of commerce to overstep the barriers
which kept the original colonies apart, and
that it was through the colleges that this
commerce was begun and maintained.

This is no small part of the benefit which Culture
American universities and colleges have con- and
Character
ferred and still confer upon the nation. The
race problem, more sternly than any other,
presses for solution. A nation is made and
maintained great, not by the number of individuals contained within its boundaries, but
by the strength that comes from common
national ideals and aspirations. No nation can
be great that is not homogeneous in this sense.
I have said, and every one who has eyes can
see, that this homogeneity is promoted by the
elementary and secondary schools; but perhaps
there is not proper appreciation of the colleges
as a constant and pervasive force that is tending
gradually to fuse the diverse racial elements
into one common nationality, having one
language, one literature, one patriotism and
one ideal of social and political development.

Progress is more often a pull than a push—
"a surging forward of the exceptional man
and the uplifting of his duller brethren slowly
and painfully to his higher level." The educated men and women of the different races
in America, with their larger vision and deeper
sensibilities, are ordinarily wise and conservative
leaders of their fellows whom they serve in a
thousand ways, giving more adequate standards
of living and loftier ideals of life to those whose
ignorance of letters is less dangerous than their
ignorance of life.

Inter-
marriages
and Race
Character-
stics.

And, in appreciable measure, they are dissipating racial prejudices. In the higher realms
of intellectual commerce, as in an oasis amid a
wide desert of caste and proscription, the best
representatives of all races meet and mingle,
aiding each other's growth and all striving, in
generous rivalry, to a high ideal; and thus
mutual respect is won. Even in the kingdom
of culture—the purest democracy in, because it
is not of, this world—the old base prejudice too
often raises its head and the heartburning jars
and slights of deep race dislike are not unknown. For race-feeling is older than intellectual development; and reason, based on larger
knowledge and experience, does not quickly
bring to the emotional life the intimate sense
of kindred humanity in which alone the super-

stitions bred of race-feeling can wholly die.
But the men of broadest reason and widest
catholicity give, and ultimately compel less
noble souls to yield, generous acknowledgment of a common humanity and a common
pursuit. At every university and college that
I have visited, I have heard ungrudging praise
of the exceptional ability of the Jewish, especially of the Russian Jewish, students—men who
went as steerage passengers from Europe and
on their arrival in America seemed, to undiscerning eyes, the most unpromising material
that any country could import. But these dry
sticks of a rotten branch, like the rod of Aaron,
and quite as miraculously, have " brought forth
buds and bloomed blossoms and yielded
almonds "; and what these have accomplished
many more will attempt in the great democracy
where, to the educated men and women of
any nation or race, all careers are open. Nor
is it unworthy of notice that statistics show
that most of the intermarriages of immigrants
of any nationality with immigrants of other
nationalities and with native-born Americans
are between the educated men and women of the
different races ; and these are found everywhere
in places of influence and authority. It is one
of the favourite theories of social philosophers
that mixed races are the best; and it is true,

as a matter of history, that the most progressive peoples of Europe are of mixed blood. The American nation of the future promises to be a new race, composed of many diverse elements ; and it is the belief of many that it will be a race not only different from, but superior to, any of the older nationalities. This, however, can only be if the constituent elements of this amalgamation are of fine quality ; and as the quality is being largely determined by the colleges which attract the best and make it better, there is reason for the hope of Americans that the fusion that is in process will produce a people possessing the highest characteristics of the several elements that unite.

The Aim of the Colleges.

The democratic character of American universities and colleges has enabled them to render this high national service. Americans, when in generalising mood, say that the German university has in mind the scholar, the English university the gentleman, and the American university and college the citizen. The generalisation, if pressed too far, becomes untrue ; but it fairly indicates that the conscious aim of the founders and supporters of American institutions of higher education has been, and is, to educate a democracy in democracy. The President of Dartmouth College has said that he would find it a congenial task to

educate the scholar after the German fashion, and
an easy task to determine the social standards
of a college through those rigid inquiries which,
he says, guard the entrance to academic life at
Oxford and Cambridge ; but that the American
task is to take the average product of a democracy and qualify as much of it as possible
for independent scholarship, mould as much of
it as possible into the habits of a gentleman,
and fit it all, by all the means and incentives at
command, for the high estate of influential
citizenship in a democracy.

The ends considered secondary are being in Its Defeat
large measure achieved ; nor is the primary by Fraternities
aim altogether missed.   But, entrenched in
American universities and colleges, are institutions called fraternities which have successfully
repulsed a general attack which has developed
against them in recent years.   These fraternities
are secret societies, based upon kindred interests
and tastes.   They bear Greek-letter names,
such as Alpha Delta Phi, Delta Kappa Epsilon,
and Psi Upsilon, which have some significance
which none but the initiated may know.   Some
fraternities have as many as seventy " chapters "
distributed through as many colleges ; and the
chapters bear to each other a relation similar to
that which exists between Masonic lodges.   In
college grounds, there are often costly chapter-

houses which provide for the fraternity members,
and exclusively for them, all that is fundamental
in the life of a young man—"a pleasant place
to sleep in and to dine, and a pleasant fellow
with whom to work and to play." Membership
of certain fraternities confers social distinction
and is greatly coveted; and, as popularity is
ordinarily the most important condition of
obtaining election, to become popular becomes
the ruling passion of many who are ambitious
of the honour. These resort to pretence sometimes; and from Yale graduates I have heard
strange tales of the sudden lapse from such
grace as membership of the Students' Christian
Association may be held to imply, on the part
of candidates who have failed of election to the
"Skull and Bones" or "Scroll and Key"
which are secret, although not Greek-letter
fraternities, and to which members are elected,
not as ordinarily from amongst the freshmen or
sophomores but from the incoming senior class,
by graduating members, on the eve of "Commencement."

Con-
cerning
Fraterni-
ties.

Fraternity members wear and display
badges of various kinds, such as a key or
a shield bearing the Greek letter-name, and
have secret hand-grips, watchwords, hailing
signs of recognition and membership tests.
Most colleges that have any, have many,

fraternities; and, at the beginning of each session, social attentions are paid, often in competition, by the members of the several societies to such freshmen as may be deemed desirable as fellow-members on account of some distinction, which is not infrequently that of wealth, which they are supposed to possess —an undignified scramble which, not inappropriately, is called "rushing." Election is for life and, after college days, close relations are maintained between graduate and undergraduate members, and any man who has been to college and cannot wear a fraternity badge has forever to overcome a certain presumption against him in the public mind. It will be interesting to consider what gave birth to these institutions, and what kind and degree of influence they have upon the life of individual students and upon corporate collegiate life.

CHAPTER XV.

COLLEGE FRATERNITIES.

"Dum vitant stulti vitia, in contraria currunt."—HORACE.
"Trust me, you have an exceeding fine lodging here—very neat and private."—BEN JONSON.

Fraternities and Sororities—Their *raison d'être*—Their manifold Evils—Their undemocratic Character — Ineffectual Attempts at Suppression—The better Way: Reconstruction—Social Life in American and some English Colleges—The Rhodes Scholars and their Task.

Fellow-
ship—
FRATERNITIES, as a strict interpretation of the name implies, are exclusively for men. But women, when they were admitted to the universities and colleges and when women's colleges were founded, set themselves to secure the advantages, such as they might be, of fraternities by organising similar institutions for themselves; and these are now found in most of the western co-educational colleges and State universities, in some colleges for women, and even in many high schools, both east and west. These are sometimes called sororities; but generally they call themselves and prefer to be called fraterni-

ties. To a Greek-letter fraternity, connected with a woman's college, I brought an introduction from a relative of mine who, not altogether unwisely, had studied American women's colleges from within as a student at one of them, and who was, and therefore is, a fraternity member. The introduction ran: "My dear Girls,—I introduce to you by this note your Uncle Alick." Curious to know whether sorority was so fully recognised in this society that my relationship to one of its members would be accepted as involving the same relationship to all her fellow-members, I forwarded the letter, with a formal covering note from myself, immediately on arrival in America. By return post, I received the reply: "Our dear Uncle Alick, Come along immediately and we will take care of you. Rushing will be in full swing soon. We want your help." I went and was taken care of; and I found, as I have found in men's fraternities, that the bonds of fellowship were many and strong.

—as enjoyed by the Author—

It was to promote social union that fraternities were first formed. They have increased in number and strength, in spite of persistent opposition, because the colleges failed to make proper provision for the social life of the students; and they became secret, partly because of a certain hostility between pro-

—is the Aim—

13

fessors and students and chiefly because the
investiture of a little mystery made them more
attractive to youthful minds : what happens, for
example, within the stone, windowless, tomb-
like halls of the "Skull and Bones" is a constant and attractive riddle to the students at
Yale.   In many colleges, the conditions which
determined the character of the original fraternities have been modified, but the original
character of these societies has persisted ; and,
although American institutions of higher education, which at first closely followed one type,
are now greatly diversified and are governed
by widely differing social, educational, moral
and political influences, yet in all kinds, and
in most of each kind, fraternities are found.
Although, as I have said, the best American
universities, for the purposes of scholarly
instruction in general and of instruction in
modern sciences in particular, are perhaps
superior, yet in all social aspects they are
inferior, to English colleges which, in this
latter respect, as Americans testify, are as
nearly perfect as human institutions are capable
of becoming.   Fraternities represent an attempt,
on the part of American students, to satisfy
their social cravings by providing in their
chapter-houses an equivalent of the English
college residential halls.

The attempt is laudable; but the result is —often defeated— necessarily inadequate and fraught with harm of to the highest interests of the students and Fraternities. colleges. At Oxford and Cambridge there are clubs; but a student who belongs to one or more of them is still bound up, in his general life, with the life of his college. The member of an American fraternity, however, is, by the very nature of its organisation, withdrawn from all of his fellow-students who are not fellow-"frats"; and his first loyalty is not to his college, but to his fraternity. The disabilities under which non-fraternity students lie are serious; and about one-third of the students are outside their college fraternities. All of these are socially unaffiliated with the college; and they lack all the facilities, social and intellectual, that come from fraternal life. This evil is found in many non-residential English universities; but in America, it is intensified by the custom, which obtains in most colleges, of organising the social life in the first year of the undergraduate's course. Thus, students who fail of election to a fraternity in their freshman year are doomed to perpetual exclusion. "Some fellows," it has been said, An American "starve physically without a friend with whom at Oxford to share their hardships; and some, after a few quoted. months of lonesomeness and neglect, give up their university career, broken-hearted, and so take perhaps their first step in a life of failure"; and even those who graduate, even if it be with honours, can never wear a fraternity badge which is ordinarily more highly prized than any distinction that is legitimately academic.

The Defeat of the Aim—seen in Members— Possibly, however, evil is subtly wrought more surely upon those who are, than upon those who are not, fraternity members. The dominant ambition of each society is to make itself strong and influential and to draw into it those who will increase its power. These are not usually the most refined and scholarly students; and their influence becomes more pernicious in the confined atmosphere in which it is exerted than it would be in the general college life. Many fraternities certainly have excellent fellows as members; but their fellowship is restricted to their own exclusive set and thus they lose the great benefit that should come from familiar association in college with many dissimilar minds. And, in their "rushes" to secure the most coveted members, and especially in their combinations in favour of the fraternities as against the colleges, these societies give rise to some of the most disturbing and belittling factors of college life. There are one or two fraternities to which these strictures do not apply. The Phi Beta Kappa, for example, has chapters in most universities; but, it has no dormitory buildings or dining halls, it is not primarily social, and it is not a secret society. Its members are elected by the University Faculty for excellence in proper academic work; and as long as the ordinary "pass" degree is no real distinction, such a fraternity will have a legitimate place in the academic life of the nation. The other is, however, the prevailing kind; and I have not overstated the evils to which it gives rise.

But the chief objection urged by American opponents of fraternities is that they are un-democratic and tend to emphasise social distinctions and foster cliques. Even in so aristocratic a country as Germany, students meet upon terms of fraternal equality: a common devotion to knowledge, without destroying the distinctions of birth and fortune, creates above them a higher university where the most intelligent and laborious take the first place. American colleges and universities fall below this level; and perhaps their greatest need is a purer and better democracy in which there shall be neither need nor place for the present social organisations and combinations which reproduce the class distinc-

—and in general College Life.

tions based chiefly on wealth which are arising in all parts of the country.

Bold Reforms.

Many attempts have been made to suppress fraternities. But opposition has only served to make them more secret, and perhaps to change their name to clubs. Princeton prohibited them in 1853; and to-day that university is honeycombed with clubs which cause heartburnings by their exclusiveness, break up the solidarity of the students and interfere with their proper work. Now, saner methods are advocated. Recognising that fraternities persist because they supply in some measure a vital need of college life educational reformers propose to reorganise the social life of the college and provided intelligently what the students are blindly striving to secure. Educational experiments are being attempted in American universities based upon experiences in other countries and notably in England. Two years ago President Wilson introduced a modified form of the Oxford tutorial system into Princeton This reform, which marks a spirit of reaction from the advance of German methods, is being effected with ease and enthusiasm and is restoring the close and intimate contact o pupil and teacher which had been lost, with so much else that was valuable, in the rapic growth of American colleges. While this system is still in the experimental stage, President Wilson boldly addresses himself to the problem of fraternities, from which many college presidents have turned in dismay, and announces a plan to establish quadrangles at Princeton—that is, small self-contained colleges within the university, after the manner of Oxford and Cambridge, with a common living room and dining hall in which the students of all the four years shall reside together; and the President suggests that, as an act of supreme self-sacrifice, the existing clubs at Princeton, one of which owns a house valued at $100,000, should turn their property over to the university to be transformed into the new "quads." The University of Wisconsin, one of the best and most democratic State institutions, has discovered that the influence of fraternities is wholly undemocratic, and is bent upon building up a college residential life. Many years ago, President Eliot of Harvard suggested that the manifold problems that have come up with the growth and prosperity of American universities might be solved by building up colleges within each university; and now, Charles Francis Adams proposes a comprehensive scheme which, if carried into effect, would make the present

Harvard cease to exist except in continuity
and in name, the chief change being the
formation of a group of colleges, each independent and so limited in size that individuality
should be, not only possible but a necessary
part of the scheme, the students and instructors
in each constituting a large household under
several roofs and with common grounds. It
is claimed that if this plan were adopted, the
university would revert to the original idea of
the American college: it would also conform
in many respects to the present idea of the
English university on which, originally, the
American college was formed.

The Ideal
to be
realised.
In the consideration and application of these
proposals, the Rhodes scholars at Oxford from
American colleges who have come into close
personal contact with the ideals and purposes
of both the English and American systems of
education, now so widely different in their
development and applications, and who thus
can properly estimate the elements of the
strength and greatness of each, will doubtless
give effective aid.   Rhodes knew that he
builded ; but he builded better than he knew.
And the American university, when it succeeds
in combining with its present instruction the
new social life after which it is so earnestly
striving, will see the evils of fraternities and

of athletics die a natural death; will fulfil the expectations regarding it which many close and competent observers entertain; and will perhaps be, as Americans are determined that it shall become, the most perfect educational system in the history of civilisation. America looks to the Rhodes scholars for impulse and guidance to this goal.

CHAPTER XVI.

SOCIAL DISCONTENT.

"Poverty is an odious calling."—BURTON, *Anatomy of Melancholy.*

Poverty that is Clothed, but Ashamed—Some Statistics—Wage-Earners and Salary-Earners—Sensitiveness to Poverty—Contrasted with England—Mere Law-Honesty—Fettered by the Constitution—Trusts and Individualism—Legal Ethics.

The Poor.

I HAVE never indulged in the fashionable pastime of slumming. I have, however, acquaintance with the poorest quarters of most of the capitals of the world; and, in analogous districts of American cities, I have been impressed by the comparative absence of the outward and visible sign of deep and widespread poverty which is seen, by the most casual observer, in the dress of large classes of citizens in other lands. It seems as if Americans, alone of all peoples, had not the poor, at least in appreciable number, always with them.

Their Thought for Raiment.

But things are not what they seem; and the appearance of Americans is a deceptive guide to their true estate.   The poor are here.   Their democratic training, however, has led them to presuppose that a common standard belongs to all ; and to this standard they are constantly striving to conform.   It is easier for the poor to approach to conformity to the rich in their dress than in any other particular.   Therefore, the poor in America take more thought for raiment, and devote to it a larger proportion of their income, than the poor in other lands ; and the appearance of general prosperity indicates an effort towards democratic expression, rather than the universal possession of adequate means of existence.   The familiar tokens of Their low poverty are found in the homes of multitudes Estate. of those whom one sees elsewhere in brave attire.   I first made acquaintance with this fact by visiting in their homes some men and women whom I had met at social settlements ; and, later, statistics confirmed my personal view. In New York City, according to official reports, two-thirds of the inhabitants live in tenement houses that have over 350,000 living rooms into which, because they are windowless, no ray of sunlight ever comes.   In fairly prosperous years there are at least 10,000,000—some careful statisticians say from 15,000,000 to 20,000,000—people in America who are always underfed and poorly housed ; and of these,

4,000,000 are public paupers. Little children, to the number of 1,700,000, who should be at school, and about 5,000,000 women are wage-earners in America. Yet the Bureau of Labour for Wisconsin reports that less than 3 per cent. of the *families* of Wisconsin have an income of over $600, while nearly 52 per cent. live on less than $400 a year; and Lavasseur, in his book *The American Worker*, estimates the total income of all the wage-earners in an average American *family* at about $657.

Classes and Masses.

The case of "salary-earners" must also be taken into consideration. The prosperity of the country, which has brought some material benefit to wage-earners and to men of wealth, has brought no corresponding improvement in the condition of the professional class. On the contrary, hand in hand with general prosperity has come a proportionate increase in the cost of living; and the professional class—the most important element in the citizenship of the country—has not shared in the increased riches of the time. I have referred to the inadequate salaries of teachers in the primary and secondary schools. Those of college and university professors come under the same condemnation. For example, at Harvard, during the administration of its actual president, the higher salaries have, indeed, been raised 25 per cent., but the average salary has been diminished by 40 per cent. — from $3444 in 1867–8 to $2070 in 1902–3. Thus the men and women who are the real forces of the democracy find themselves, along with the wage-earners, brought face to face, in their own experience, with the tremendous modern problem of the distribution of wealth, and are in constant danger of mistaking their personal *malaise* for altruistic sympathy with mankind. And, as I have indicated, there is a large pauper class with which to sympathise. A report of the "Department of Correction" shows that one person in every ten who dies in New York has a pauper's burial; that, at the present ratio of deaths from tuberculosis, 10,000,000 persons now living will succumb to that disease, which is largely due to insufficiency of food and light and air; and that 60,463 families in the borough of Manhattan, New York, were evicted from their homes in the year 1903.

I know little of statistics; and these figures may compare favourably with those of other countries. But the poverty in America that seeks to hide itself beneath fine apparel may be more bitter and more dangerous, even although it be less than the poverty that elsewhere is naked and unashamed. At a

Their Habit of Mind.

meeting of "Christian Socialists" which I
attended at Hull House, Chicago, an Americanised Scot won the sympathy of his audience
by vehemently protesting against "the life-
long and unpardonable indignity" that had
been put upon him by those who had called
the school in Edinburgh in which he had
been fed, clad and educated, "the Ragged
Boys' School." "I will never forgive them
that word 'ragged,'" the man exclaimed.
Social settlements in America and in England
provide, without charge, legal advice for those
who need or desire it, and cannot afford to
pay a lawyer's fee; but in America no settlement ventures to wound the susceptibilities
of the recipients by announcing a "poor man's
lawyer," which is the term frankly used in
England without shadow of offence. These
things are of small moment in themselves;
but they serve to indicate the habit of mind
that prevails—a habit that is not without its
dangers; for are we not apt to hold ourselves
dispossessed of whatever we are reluctant to
acknowledge ourselves unpossessed? Lasalle
complained that, in Germany, the industrial
classes were so insensible to their indigence
that the first indispensable task of Socialists
was to teach them their misery. This pre-
liminary work is not necessary in America.

The indigent are more than sensible of, they are sensitive to, their lack.

In America, as is generally known, there is great concentration of wealth. Twenty per cent. of the entire wealth of the country is owned by three one-hundredths of 1 per cent. of the population ; and the total number of millionaires in New York City alone rose from 28 to 1103 between the years 1885–92. Some of these fortunes have been well won and others ill won ; but nice discriminations are not made in the popular judgment upon the possessors of great wealth ; and those whose fortunes have been made as an incident to performing great services to the community are victims of the general resentment which has been aroused by those who have fraudulently grown rich. And it must be admitted that the goats would probably be found to outnumber the sheep if any unerring separation were made, at least if those were included among the unrighteous whose righteousness did not exceed that of the "merely law-honest," to adopt President Roosevelt's term. And, indeed, law-honesty in money-making may, in America, cover many acts which the law of other lands— leaving out of consideration the tribunal which has higher than human sanctions—and

The popular Estimate of Men of Wealth.

the public conscience in America, as elsewhere, treat as crimes.

Nor can Americans easily bring their law
into closer agreement with their conscience.
They are held in fetters forged by their
forefathers in the very act which these
thought had guaranteed that they and their
posterity should be forever free.   In the
endeavour to prevent any intrusion into the
domain of individual activity they encased the
powers of the State, local and national, in a
system of constitutional limitations unprecedented in the history of the world; and
an unforeseen effect has been to provide
private corporations with peculiar vantage
ground, by giving them such immunity from
State control as has never been guaranteed
to them by English law or by Roman law as
administered in Europe.   A decision of the
Supreme Court, in what is known as the
Dartmouth College case, made the situation
plain.   It was then held that the charter of
a private corporation is a contract within the
meaning of that clause in the United States
Constitution which declares that no State
shall make any law impairing the law of
contracts.   This has secured "Trusts" immunity from State control; and thus they
have been able to give the rein to their

dominating impulse to organise and con-
solidate, within and beyond the limits of
"mere law-honesty," so that the will and
identity of the individual worker, in every
department of life, should be obliterated and
lost in aggregations which swallow up all
minor competitors.   This is the elimination
of individualism as the foundation of the
national life; and this evil, wrought by
capitalists, is the very head and front of
the offending with which, by capitalists,
Socialism is charged.

The battle against "predatory wealth," no —a Fight
less than that against Socialism, is a fight for
for the very life of the nation.   It is sure to National
be a long and hard struggle; for legal skill Life—
has combined with wealth to defraud and
despoil the public, even in defiance and
contempt of law.   "We all know," President
Roosevelt said recently at Harvard, "we all
know that as things actually are many of the
most influential and most highly remunerated
members of the Bar in every centre of wealth
make it their special task to work out bold
and ingenious schemes by which their wealthy
clients, individual or corporate, can evade the
laws which were made to regulate, in the
interests of the public, the uses of wealth."
Let Harvard take the hint.   Legal ethics

14

receive scant attention in American university law schools—at Yale, merely five lectures in a three years' course; at Chicago, merely lectures which are relegated to the "non-credit courses"; and at Harvard, as at Columbia, no recognition at all.

CHAPTER XVII.

SOCIALISM.

"They made me the keeper of the vineyards; but mine own vineyards have I not kept."—THE SONG OF SOLOMON.

Presumptions against the Rich—Munificence or Restitution?—
Unchivalrous *Fainéants* — Theological and Sociological
Readjustments — Marxian Calvinism — A Confession of
Faith—The Prospects of Socialism in America.

THUS wealth has developed without any Million-
proportionate development of the moral, aires in
social and legal sanctions by which its pursuit, repute—
possession and use ought to be controlled.
Consequently, in America, a rich man lies
under such presumptions and prejudices that
he must prove himself innocent before he is
believed to be guiltless of malpractices in the
acquisition of his wealth; and the opportunity
of proof is even less frequently given than
sought. This prejudice is not confined to the
very poor and very ignorant. I happened to
be in correspondence with a college while I
was the guest of a reputed millionaire—a
friend of many years. When I got to the

college and was amongst the professors, I, who
alone knew my friend, was alone in believing
him to be an honourable man ; and my belief,
I fear, was suspected to be merely from the
teeth outwards—professed on account of the
hospitality that I had received.   So it is
everywhere in America, and I have not found
it so elsewhere.

—not
vithout
Reason. Nor are these prejudices softened by the
great gifts to education and charity which fall
upon the nation in golden showers from the
coffers of millionaires.   Their moral title to
their gold is challenged, and their charity is
cynically interpreted as an attempt, by the
restitution of a part, to compensate for injustice
in gaining the whole.   The generous bene-
factors are living in a fool's paradise if they
imagine that their gifts awaken public gratitude
towards themselves and their class.   I have
sometimes thought that colleges, libraries and
other buildings bearing their donors' names,
from the sight of which one cannot escape,
tend in the present popular mood to keep the
public mind inflamed.   Often I heard the
couplet quoted—

> "Who builds a church to God and not to fame
> Will never mark the marble with his name";

and, because I strive to cultivate restraint in

speech, the language used by the *alumni* of colleges with reference to names of millionaires imposed upon "donated" buildings must go unreported by me. Nor does it go unnoticed that the rich do not give *themselves* to the public service or the general welfare. Some of them have intellectual and moral sanity and refinement, and do not seem to lack the specifically social qualities, virtues and amenities which are supposed to be the exclusive possession of an hereditary aristocracy. Even these men, however, with one or two notable exceptions, are unchivalrous *fainéants* in relation to the social and political problems that press for solution ; and the baser sort, more completely, I think, than the analogous class of any other country are content, in heartlessness and selfishness, to follow the thoughtless pursuits and conventions of their "set," in which the greatest consideration is given to those who have amassed enough wealth to rank amongst multi-millionaires. They are, undoubtedly, a powerful class ; but their power is largely unsocial, a solvent of society and a disintegrating force in the national life, in spite of, and sometimes even by reason of, occasional bequests to "endow a college or a cat." The gift without the giver is bare ; and the rich as a class will remain in disrepute as long as they remain so absorbed in becoming richer, or in spending or even giving their wealth, that they cannot take their proper part, without fear or favour, in the tasks which, in a democracy, no individual can honourably avoid.

'ondition nd Creed.

These sharp social contrasts and divisions were not always found in the New World. In the early days of New England, a rhymster, accounted a poet, wrote, ungrammatically and perhaps untruthfully, that all the people dwelt

> "Under thatch'd huts, without the cry of rent,
> And the best sauce to every dish—content."

"We are all freeholders" was the proud message sent back to England by one of the settlers. "Rent day doth not trouble us; and all good blessings we have in their season for the taking." This release, enjoyed in measure for generations, from the hard pressure of European life—its great cities, its dense crowds, its mean competitions and its fierce temptations—produced general social contentment, and there supervened a complacent view of human nature in which the grim doctrines of human depravity, elaborated by Augustine amid the corruptions of a decadent Rome, and by Calvin in the days of the Medicis, and imported by the Puritans, seemed far removed from truth as taught by actual fact in the New World. Accordingly, in course of time, Calvinism was dethroned, in

New England at least, by Unitarianism which, in its ultimate analysis, is distinguished by its insistence on human nature as essentially good ; and the supporters of this new theology confidently expected that, as a matter of course, it would establish itself everywhere in the New World as a positive and commanding faith. In course of time, however, and in proportion as America reproduced the social conditions of Europe, it was seen, in the result, that human nature remained the same in the New World as in the Old. And later attempts to make an adjustment between theology and the facts of life led to a return, not indeed to the old Calvinism, but to the old doctrines of human sin and Divine grace.

But sociologists, as well as theologians, felt the need of adjusting theory to fact; and, under the pressure of the new social conditions, they imported from Europe the doctrine known as Socialism, and especially that form of it advocated by Karl Marx. According to Marx, "the manner of production for man's material life determines (*bedingt*) the social, political and mental life. It is not the mind of man that determines his life; it is this life that determines mind." This, which is perilously near the doctrine that *Mann ist was er isst*, is the essential element of Marxian Socialism—

Calvinism in Sociology.

its materialistic conception of history. It is materialism applied to history. According to materialism, everything is the result of necessary movements of matter, everything is *determined* in a link of causation. According to Marxism, everything, even religion, is *determined* by social conditions, and Socialism is predetermined and is as certain as the rising and setting of the sun. Lo! here are the familiar terms of Calvinism; and, in fact, the Socialist, so far as he is Marxian and materialistic, is, as some one has said, a Calvinist—without God: a distinction with a tremendous difference! And, curiously enough, the method and style of Karl Marx carry us back to the ecclesiastical schoolmen. His *Das Kapital* has been called, not inappropriately, the sacred book of Socialism; and I have found Jews who reverence it as a new Torah, and Gentiles who accept it as a new Gospel. They do not understand it, as I confess that I do not; probably they have not even read it. But what of that? *Credo ut intelligam.*

A Confession of Faith. If it be true, as Karl Marx asserts, that Socialism is a necessary product of capitalism, and if, as Stahl maintains, Socialism is an inevitable corollary of democracy, it follows that America, which is a democracy and has the highest capitalistic development, must also be the classic land of Socialism, and its labouring class must take the lead in the most radical Socialist movement. But I, too, would test theory by facts; and therefore I gave myself, in America, to Socialist leaders, Socialist literature and Socialist meetings with such constant devotion that any who judged me by the company that I kept, possibly concluded that I was devoted to Socialism itself. And as the opinions of an observer regarding the growth and strength of any movement are apt to be influenced by his personal beliefs, it is due to any by whom my reflections may be read that I should state that I neither accept the Socialist's programme nor share the Socialist's aim. I believe that, as Aristotle says, virtue consists in avoiding the too little and the too much; and I equally distrust rigid revolutionary conservatism and reckless revolutionary radicalism, both of which, as it seems to me, risk the treasures painfully accumulated during many years of progress by the human race. If, indeed, Socialism meant enthusiasm for humanity, fervent desire for and endeavour after the highest welfare of every human being —and that is the true meaning of the term —then I should humbly claim the wish to be a Socialist. But the term has been

degraded from its true significance and made
to mean an economic system in which private
capital shall be prohibited and the State shall
own all the means of production. Such a
Socialism is "a matter of kitchen and scullery,"
and I repudiate it. The true economic task,
as I apprehend, is to teach the meaning and
function of material possessions, so that all
may realise in what true wealth and true
life consist. When this lesson has been
learned, the conflict between capital and
labour will cease, and we shall see the
ministration of every class to every other
class in a democracy that lifts all and humbles
none. The most precious thing in the world
is the individual mind and soul with unfettered
capacity for service and growth; and while
I am painfully sensible of the great evils
wrought under the present economic system,
I would not seek to remove them by the
system of Socialism, which, in order that
the ends of mediocrity might be served, would
hold the best minds and souls in check,
denying them full political, social and moral
utterance, and so would irretrievably reduce
the true wealth of nations, as well as the
"abundance of *things*," in which neither
individual nor national life "consists."

Faith and
light.

I ask myself what effect upon myself as

an observer of facts my personal opinions
upon Socialism have had ; and I answer—
the ordinary effect of dislike and fear. I
am predisposed to see Socialism where it is
not, rather than not to see it where it is,
and to overestimate, rather than to under-
estimate, its growth and strength. Yet the
conclusion has been forced upon me that
Socialism has found, finds and is fated to
find, in the American democracy, uncongenial
soil. If this be a just conclusion, it confutes
the theory, which many accept, that Socialism
must have its speediest and its highest
development wherever there is the highest
capitalistic development; the Marxian "inevitable future" is disproved by the facts.
There can be no more important work for
the statesman or the sociologist than to fathom
this phenomenon. But merely to state, not
to fathom it, is my modest part. "*Je n'impose
rien, je ne propose même rien ; j'expose.*"

CHAPTER XVIII.

SOCIALISM AND DEMOCRACY.

"On the strong and cunning few
Cynic favours I will strew,
I will stuff their maw with overplus until their spirit dies."
WILLIAM VAUGN MOODY.

Socialist Political Parties—German and Russian Socialists—
The Foreign Vote—No Distinctions exist, but not a
Class System—This Social Equality a Bulwark against
Socialism—Defection of Americanised Immigrants from
Socialism — Socialism and Liberty — Socialist "Intel-
lectuals" — The Universities and Socialism — Social
Struggle not mere Class Strife.

Socialism
a Factor,
but not a
Menace,—

TWO of the political parties in America are organised on a Socialistic basis; and at the last Presidential election they cast 453,338 votes. This figure may be accepted as representing their full strength at that time. Owing to the confusion of issues at that election, and the tendency of all Americans, except extremists such as Socialists, to subordinate measures to men in their considerations at all elections, many undoubtedly voted the Socialist "ticket" who would not, in any circumstances, support the Socialist programme; and these, probably, were numerically equivalent to those convinced Socialists who were willing but unable to go to the polls. Now, 453,338 is an imposing figure. Yet it represents only a small fraction of the number of qualified voters, and one-half of 1 per cent. of the population, of the United States. It indicates that while Socialism has a place and is not without force in American politics, it has not gained a foothold that need cause alarm, although its presence should cause vigilance, on the part of those citizens who consider Socialism a menace to national life. —in America— The important question relates to the future. In America, do present social conditions and the present condition of Socialism indicate the triumph, or do they presage the defeat, of Socialistic propagandism? The conclusion is not so clear that it can be enunciated in a definite form. The utmost which can be safely hazarded is to relate honestly such facts as I seem to have observed, and to refrain as far as possible from judicial sentence upon them.

Socialists find their best recruiting ground —in amongst recent immigrants; and this makes Virtue of De-Socialism especially formidable at elections. mocracy having Under "universal suffrage" adult males, and secured— only they, are qualified to vote; and as the "foreign-born" have an abnormal proportion of adults and of males, the numerical strength of the "native-born" in the population is not fully represented by their strength at the polls. Excluding negroes from our calculations, we find from the census returns of 1880 that the native-born and foreign-born males of twenty-one years and over constitute, the former only 22·4 per cent. and the latter as much as 46 per cent. of their respective populations. Owing to the short period required for naturalisation, the adult immigrants early acquire votes, and perhaps the majority of them incline to Socialism in the first years of their citizenship. Germans and Russians have probably been avowed and active Socialists in the countries which they have left. Until recently this easy and rapid increase of the foreign vote has excited little apprehension; but now the question is often asked whether the continuous incorporation by the body politic of these multitudes of voters who have had no training in self-government does not tend to weaken the political capacity of the nation and to prevent the proper adjustment of democratic institutions to the expanding national life. Certainly, the policy hitherto pursued has not been unattended by grave dangers; yet it may be held to be justified by its results. It has

—to Immigrants—

been one of the most powerful forces tending to preserve the measure of social equality which America has always enjoyed; and this, in turn, has preserved the State from Socialistic schemes.

Of course, there have been from the beginning, and there are, social distinctions. In the beginning, the social hierarchy was based on education, public service and the acknowledged importance of the ministers of religion. Till 1885 the Quinquennial Catalogues of Harvard University marked with italics the names of graduates who had attained the dignity of ministers, and with capital letters the names of such as had become Governors or Judges. Those were the "quality" of that time. As the complexity of the national life developed, the squire, the lawyer and the doctor gained social consideration and maintained careful observance of the social tradition. And, from the first, a certain inferiority attached to those who never reached intellectual eminence and to immigrant servants and their descendants. Yet, all enjoyed equally all the dignity that is given by a vote in a democratic community; and this prevented the growth, not of classes, but of a well-defined system of classes and of a servile class; and this policy, persistently pursued to the present

—Social Equality.

day in relation to immigrants, has maintained this measure of social equality. This, in turn, has proved a bulwark against Socialism.

Equality— For Socialism, as Americans have been quick to recognise, would have, as one of its first and most disastrous effects, the creation of such class distinctions as the democracy has hitherto abjured. To give inefficient or unfortunate groups of people a claim upon the labour of other and more efficient or more fortunate groups, would be to introduce the oldest kind of inequality based upon the old claim of privilege ; and I have found American citizens, and not only those of them that are rich, as ready to oppose any claim of privilege on the ground of poverty as they have always been to resist the claim when it has been offered on the ground of rank and birth.

—as Immigrants recognise— Immigrants, when they become American citizens, quickly take pride in and bravely shoulder the responsibilities and results of their new *status*. By their migration, they severed the ties by which they were pulled down in the countries which they left; and they make no demand for other ties by which they may be pulled up. Their demand is for opportunity to rise by their own efforts; and that, in large and ever-increasing measure, as free men in a free democracy they have.

Consequently, the Socialism which they had embraced in their native countries or on their arrival in America, they tend to renounce in proportion as they become Americanised; and the Socialists' ranks would quickly show the effect of this process were they not perpetually reinforced by new immigrants whom, in turn, they lose and, in turn, replace. The defection of Russians and Germans is especially decided and rapid. In the countries which they have left, the economic conditions of Socialism exist, but political rather than economic conditions are favourable to its growth; and the increase of Socialism in Russia and Germany has been largely due to the presence of revolutionary elements that have been bred in the long struggle for political emancipation. In America, the economic conditions favourable to Socialism undoubtedly exist; but they exist only in a greatly modified form and the revolutionary element does not exist at all; and the socialistic doctrines imported to the New World have not the success which they gain in the Old.

Freedmen value freedom above all else; —and Liberty— and the immigrants, who became free on incompatible their advent to the free democracy, test with Socialism, as all else, by the degree to which Socialism. it guarantees liberty. To them, liberty is not a means to equality or any other social end.

15

There are, to them, no major considerations for which liberty may be impaired. And, rather more than less than others, they are quick to understand that, in the absence of equality of ability and efficiency, the socialistic scheme of universal economic equality could only be effected at the cost of individual liberty. The equality of opportunity in liberty for which the democracy stands, they demand; but the equality of conditions, by compulsion, in servitude, which Socialism stands for, they renounce. The most effective opponent of Socialism, as of many other ills, in America is democracy. And perhaps a more menacing evil than Socialism is what I have called the elective despotism to which I have frequently referred and under which the Constitution is being changed by a show of constitutional means—as happened in Athens where the phantom of democracy was long maintained by a body of 5000 which never met. The Republic is imperilled in proportion as its democratic character is lost. The cure for the ills of democracy is more democracy.

Wanted— a Leader. Socialism was imported to America by Germans in the seventies when the Labour Party was formed, and for fifteen years it was in America, as it has been described, a mere episode of German Socialism. In recent years,

however, considerable headway has been made
among native-born Americans, owing partly
to the social conditions which I described, and
which, if they were not created, were at least
promoted in their growth, by immigration.
But Socialists, in their eagerness to disprove
the charge that they are an alien party, are
apt to claim and proclaim as of their number
all native-born Americans who so much as
hold that the present industrial organisation
is not in correspondence with their idea of
right, or who even express generous sympathy
with the poor man's case. In a current
magazine there is an article on "Socialist
'Intellectuals,'" in which the names of some
whom I had the privilege of meeting—
James B. Reynolds, Charles B. Stover, Miss
Jane Addams, and Mrs. Robbins—have prominent place. These are eminent and influential Americans who would be a tower
of strength to any cause. I found, in each
of them, a vivid sense of justice, vital and
far-reaching human sympathy, deep pity for
sorrow and suffering, and genuine enthusiasm
for social reform; but I do not think that any
one of them is a Socialist. In claiming such
as these, Socialists perhaps show that they
realise that a great personality is their most
pressing need. Many foremost men show

theoretical and platonic interest in their creed ; but I did not find any man in their ranks who has impressed himself upon the national mind as an intellectual or moral force. I know Socialists in England who have the rare power of dispersing the conventional acceptations by which men live on easy terms with themselves and of obliging them to examine the grounds of their social and moral opinions ; but I do not know, or know of, one in America who can give this *höchst angenehmer Schmerz* which must precede any great political or economic change.

If, however, the term "intellectuals" covers all who have had a college career, a considerable number of them may be said to have professed Socialism. Socialist societies have established themselves at the universities ; and Secretary Taft, speaking at Yale, referred somewhat scornfully to these "dreamers and impracticable thinkers at the universities of this country who would abandon the system lying at the base of modern society." Well, youth everywhere is prone to be full of impetuosity and self-confidence, at once purblind and bold ; and, in its state of half-culture, undergraduate youth is peculiarly apt to seize with enthusiasm upon a general principle, regardless of its limitations or relations to other principles. But I met not a few professors

The Disqualification of Professors.

who hold and teach socialistic doctrines; and
it is significant that most, certainly the most
extreme, of these have positions in colleges
and universities which have received large
pecuniary gifts from millionaires. Influences
are subtly operating to prevent these men
from seeing truly and seeing harmoniously, or
from expressing truly and harmoniously what
they see. The trustees of the Leland-Stanford
and other privately endowed universities en-
deavoured at one time to subject their professors to doctrinal tests in political economy;
and everywhere I heard unpleasant stories of
dismissal from positions in such seats of
learning on account of "advanced" views
upon social and political questions. Doubtless
there has been exaggeration; but it has laid
upon professors the necessity of proving that
they have not surrendered their independence.
If this does not unconsciously incline them to
opinions contrary to those which are popularly
supposed to be acceptable to the wealthy bene-
factors of their institutions, it does at least lead
them to express, with conscious emphasis, such
heterodox conclusions as, by purely intellectual
processes, they may have reached, and to do
so without having previously fused and combined their material according to the laws of
what is practicable. On the other hand, those

who oppose the socialistic creed, men like
Chancellor Day, of Syracuse University, are
popularly suspected of the not wholly unworthy
motive of gratitude for past favours, or of the
wholly ignoble motive of gratitude for favours
to come; and their teaching falls on deaf ears.

The men of wealth who lavish their
gifts upon institutions of learning may be
disinterested in their effort to promote
education; and, doubtless, they have their
reward.   But their reward does not include
any increased public regard for the rights
of property. These, indeed, their pecuniary
gifts tend to jeopardise rather than safeguard.
Mr. Andrew Carnegie, in whose favour the
utmost admission that I could secure was
that, perhaps, he acquired his fortune by less
objectionable methods than those of some other
prominent capitalists, recently founded a Professors' Pension Fund, by which university
and college teachers are to be henceforth
consoled, in their economic feebleness in old
age, by the benisons of wealth to which no
direct contribution has been made by themselves.   One professor, who is already entitled,
refuses to become a beneficiary of this fund.
He has publicly declared that he would die
in his own poverty rather than accept an
outdoor relief that rested on the doctrine

The dis-
qualifying
Cause.

that the labours of the mass of men, "even educated men," are not sufficient to relieve them from charity. It is not anticipated, however, that many, if any, others will decline to feed at the crib which, by Mr. Carnegie's generosity, will be perpetually supplied; and consequently greater intensity and wider sweep will be given to the prevalent suspicion that professors are influenced by illegitimate considerations, whether they defend or whether they oppose the present industrial system on which, it is supposed, the endowments of their colleges and their own prospective pensions depend. Thus these institutions and these men are being disqualified for their high vocation of dealing authoritatively with the great problems on the solution of which the national destiny in great measure depends. One definite influence, however, the Socialist "intellectuals" exert. They tend to prevent the social struggle from degenerating into a mere class strife between organised labour and organised private capital; and class divisions, class antagonisms, class hatreds, and even class consciousness are not becoming intensified as the contentions over social questions become more intense. And I think that one hears less of the rights of working men and more of the rights of men in America than in England.

CHAPTER XIX.

SOCIAL PROGRESS.

"I have no answer for myself or thee,
Save that I learned beside my mother's knee:
'All is of God that is and is to be:
And God is good.' Let this suffice us still,
Resting in childlike trust upon His will,
Who moves to His great ends unthwarted by the ill."

WHITTIER.

American Conservatism — Diffusion of Wealth — Discontent rooted in Hope, not Fear—Proletariat and *Bourgeoisie*— A true Conception of the State—Nationalism—Ideals of the People—Relative not absolute Error—The national Destiny—From high to higher Civilisation.

Unreadiness to test untested Theories

CONSERVATISM has been declared, by all competent observers, to be a characteristic of the American democracy ; and this shows itself sometimes in regard to petty customs which do not affect the vitality of the State and always in respect of all great principles, written or unwritten, on which society, as it is organised, is based. The general political habits of the people have made them rigidly practical and have strengthened their aversion from sweeping and untried solutions of any problems. An American writer has said of them that in no way do they more clearly declare their English origin than by the serenity with which they forbid logic to meddle with the substantial maintenance of legal institutions, and defend customs which at least have proved tolerable against theory which has never been put to the test.

This was said without special reference, but it has its application, to Socialism. The economic condition of the American working man, far from satisfactory as we have seen it to be, is at least tolerable, if only because it is not hopeless. Much of his discontent springs from his hopes and not from such fears as provoke disturbance in other lands. In spite of the "Trusts," and, occasionally, even by their aid, capital is falling into the hands of an ever-increasing number of people. There is a wide and widening diffusion of it, even amongst the working classes, in the shape of stocks and bonds. Statistical *data* are incomplete, but such as are available show that the securities of the great corporations are scattered among a great and growing number of shareholders. Not only are the propertied classes not diminishing, they are increasing both relatively and absolutely ; and a vast majority

—actual Condition not being hopeless.

of the people may make their own the lines
which were aptly quoted to me by an American
working man with whom I had been discussing
the social conditions and prospects of his
class :—

> "Fortune, you say, flies from us ? She but circles
> Like the fleet sea-bird round the fowler's skiff—
> Lost in the mist one moment, and the next
> Brushing the white sail with her whiter wing,
> As if to court the aim. Experience watches
> And has her on the wing."

And as the changes in the law and the economic
situation which are actually in process conduce
to a still wider dispersion of property, the
temptation to force distribution by socialistic
reconstruction is being farther removed from
the working classes, which grow ever more
reluctant to endanger either their present
possessions or their present hopes. And, to
the dismay of the early Socialists, there has
sprung up a new and influential class, whose
members have one foot in the camp of the
proletariat and the other in the camp of the
bourgeoisie.

Immi-
grants gain
a new—

Sometimes in Germany, often in Russia, and
more than once in America amongst recent
Russian immigrants, I have heard the notorious
statement of the Communistic manifesto that
the proletarian has no fatherland quoted with
fervent approval. Russian Socialists are, as

German Socialists in the forties were, a party
of revolution, not of reform. Their aim is
radically to alter, even to abolish, the State;
and partial reforms that make conditions more
tolerable meet with their sternest opposition,
since they weaken that antagonism within the
present order that might drive society to
reconstruction on a socialistic basis. For a
time, immigrants are prone to use, in their
new land, the old arguments, in the old phrases,
of their old lands where Socialists use the term
"State," as they use the term "Capital," in a
technical sense peculiar to themselves. There,
Socialists are democrats who live in a State
which is undemocratic and stands for a class
whose interests it promotes by repressive
measures designed to keep every other class
down. They, therefore, fear the State and look
with disfavour upon plans to extend, or even
maintain, its economic functions. In America,
however, immigrants soon discover that the
political institution of the State is democratic
and can be readily made to serve the interests
of all classes, without radical political changes.
Gradually, they shed their peculiar tenets in
a land where the very premises of their arguments are lacking. Even if they continue to
profess themselves Socialists, they drop the
old revolutionary ideas and terms, and regard

the State as a positive agency for securing to
all classes and individuals in the nation the
rights which they are entitled to possess, and
especially for providing a ladder of education
and opportunity on which, if he be capable,
the humblest citizen may rise to the topmost
rung—a *Cultur-Staat* in distinction from a
Rechts-Staat or *Polizei-Staat*.

—and
true—

Properly guarded, this is a true conception
of the State. It avoids the error of attributing
to the State a separate entity, endowed with
conscience, power and will, sublimated above
human limitations and constituting a tutelary
genius over all who are subject to its authority ;
and while it recognises that the State is, as it
has been described, All-of-Us, it recognises also
that it is All-of-Us united into a moral whole
which multiplies a millionfold the aggregate
of the powers of each. The demand which
I heard from a hundred Socialist platforms,
that the State should guarantee equal rights
to all, proved to refer to equal chances, not equal
things, to all ; and this, which is not necessarily
socialistic, is the utmost demand that is made
by many who suppose that they have adopted
the Socialists' creed. And when immigrants
discover that the American State, in large and
ever-increasing measure, provides this equal
chance to all, they turn from the dislike of

patriotism and the national spirit to an acknowledgment of national interests, and from hatred
of the State to appreciation of all that government as organised in an individualistic democracy
can do for all classes ; and they identify themselves with the State which at first they had
assailed, not knowing what they did.

Herr Sombart regretfully reports to his —Con-
fellow-Socialists in Germany that, in America, the State.
the centrifugal force that leads to class hatreds
is weak, while the centrifugal force that leads
to endorsement of the national political
commonwealth—to patriotism—is strong ; and
he concludes that consequently there is a lack
among American Socialists of " that enmity
to the State so characteristic of Continental
European Socialists." This, I believe, is
sober truth. If there is any American type
of Socialism, it is Nationalism. It does not
present Socialism as a class movement. It
hopes to avoid class struggles. It is nearer
the Bernstein than the Marxian wing of the
Social democracy. It hopes to see its ideal
fulfilled through the extension of co-operation,
not through the assumption of direct control
of all production by a central political power.

Even the evils which flourish in the Politics
American State seem to moderate the of the
Socialists' aims ; and not infrequently I heard Soul.

extremists asked with some alarm, in view o
the prevalent political corruption, who is tc
guarantee the integrity of the officers in whose
hands, in the Socialistic State, political anc
economic control would be centred? A mos
pertinent inquiry! For even if the function:
of government were reduced to the lowes
term compatible with Socialism, the official:
would still have tremendous powers anc
tremendous temptations to betray their trust
and, however they might be selected anc
approved, they would still have the commor
frailties of humanity. You cannot overcome
by adding together the individual imperfec
tions of men. Behind political economy lie,
personal character. Not Socialism, or any
outward readjustment, but the inner life o
Socialists and all other citizens, is the ultimate
fact of the human problem. The true politics
as Socrates said, is first of all a politics of the
soul. And it is pleasant to be able to adc
that American Socialism has turned fron
materialism. I was much in the company o
Socialists during my year in the country; anc
I can say that I found Socialists, as a class
essentially moral and religious, opposing, some
times, organised Christianity but nearly alway
advocating the religion of Jesus as it was, no
unworthily, interpreted by themselves. Fev

of them are so blind to historical and actual
phenomena as to believe the Marxian doctrine
that everything, even religion, is merely a
product of economic life.   Even those of them
who repudiate the churches recognise religion
as an independent force, and the Christian
religion as a beneficent force, sufficient to
modify and even shape economic conditions;
and as often from Socialist platforms as from
Christian pulpits I have heard powerful
appeals to ethical sentiment.   Nor can it be
truthfully said that, among Socialists, attacks
upon the binding character of the marriage
tie in the absence of love, or after love has
disappeared, are more frequent in speech or
act than among other classes in the State.

This is all to the good.   Every class needs, A
above all else, ideals; and any class, in such terminological
mistakes as it may make in its forward effort, Inexactitude.
will be less disastrously mistaken in proportion
as it possesses a vigorous morality.   But all
this reveals a departure, not necessarily from
Socialism, but from the non-ethical Socialism
of Karl Marx, which at first was the predominant, if not the only, type.   And, in fact,
many who are classed as Socialists ought to
be called social reformers.   In common with
Socialists, they do not believe, as I who am
no Socialist do not believe, that the highest

forms of material progress can be evolved
through any merciless competition that is out
of harmony with Christian idealism and at
variance with every great system of ethics;
and they strive, as many citizens who are not
Socialists are striving, for the overthrow of
every combination of force and craft that, as
its end or its means, seeks to thrust weakness
into a yawning pit that it may ineffectually
struggle there, in black darkness, for breath
and life. But they do not find in Socialism
any panacea for all social ills. They hold
that, because society is many and complex,
the remedies of its evils must be numerous
and various, with a thousand modifications
nicely adjusted to the thousand varieties of
circumstances, situations and characters of
the individuals to whom they are applied.
And while they recognise the duty of the
State to the individual, they do not overlook
the duty of the individual to the State; nor
do they forget the supreme duty of the
individual to himself. And while they strive
for all that solidarity can give, they strive also
for all that may develop individuality. They
may be, and in my humble judgment many
of them are, in grave error as regards the
particular remedies of existing evils that they
propose; but theirs is the relative error of the

social reformer, not the absolute error of the Socialist.

The immediate danger, some fear, is that the State, exaggerating the strength of Socialism, shall become socialistic and, by summoning Beelzebub to cast out devils, subject itself to their prince. This fear is often no more than the nervousness of confused thinkers who apprehend an approach to Socialism in any measure which, in any direction and on any principle, extends the functions of the State—even in measures that have as their aim and effect the increase of individualism by the suppression of the tyranny of consolidated corporate wealth organised to obliterate the will and identity of the individual toiler in every department of life. Yet there are, perhaps, to be found in the words of some legislators and the Acts of some legislatures, possibly in reaction from excessive energy, signs of a desire to secure, by socialistic measures, absolute quiescence for every citizen, in a provision for the easy gratification, without personal effort, of all the wants of each. That achievement would, of course, create a society from which would quickly disappear patience, courage, perseverance, sympathy and other high qualities of the soul, any one of which is worth all the universe of material things—

The Conclusion of the whole Matter.

would disappear also all possibility of even
material progress, since the soul of all improvement is the improvement of the soul.   But the
national mind is sane and the national heart
is sound.   Americans, like other men, are
endowed, not only with selfish instincts but
also with instincts which prompt them to curb
their selfishness when it would disturb the
balance between the body and the soul and
between the individual and the community in
which he lives; and while many citizens will
continue to be swept into the backwaters of
Socialism, the State will continue in the
natural order of progress, preventing, not
selfishness but selfishness in excess, and
leaving, to all, the perpetual stimulus of their
individual and social instincts to still higher
civilisation under the influence of that religion
which alone of all forces has power to give
beauty of the inward soul and make the outward and inward be at one.

APPENDIX I.

THE following letter to the Editor of the *Times* contains no word of commendation of American Universities with which the author of the article to which reference is made does not heartily agree :—

"SIR, — The many American students of English institutions will read with great interest the article in the *Times* of to-day under the title, 'A Year amongst Americans.' Your correspondent's strictures on the form of the elective system adopted by some of the Universities, and more especially his condemnation of certain aspects of college athletics, will, I think, meet with the hearty approval of the great majority of the college graduates in America. Nor will they be disposed to object to his generous statement that the American Universities have elements of strength and greatness that the older English Universities lack. It would have been extremely interesting to learn what, in your correspondent's judgment, those elements are. May I suggest as among the number the following, chosen somewhat at random :—

"1. The very liberal provision for all branches of study, and the extent to which the colleges

have rid themselves of the idea that culture
comes exclusively from any one course. Cambridge is not illiberal in what she offers, but
most of her more recently established triposes
attract only a handful. In America almost
every subject finds somewhere a large number
of devotees ; and it would require some research
to discover which is the most popular.

" 2. The endeavour to keep pace with the
actual needs of the day. By this I do not
mean that ' bread-and-butter ' studies are wholly
predominant, or that a narrow utilitarianism
prevails. This common English view is
simply false. I am glad to say that the best
Universities do not neglect those studies that
play the leading parts in the older Universities.
Indeed, a very earnest endeavour is made to
make such studies of living interest. At the
same time, they do not absorb all the intellectual energy of the American student, nor
even the greater part of it. Modernism is
in the saddle, and whatever may be the
disadvantages of such a state of affairs, it
interests thousands in the Universities who
would otherwise be apathetic, and makes it
possible to provide liberally for the prosecution
of all branches of learning.

" 3. Very great attention is paid to organisation, and the administration of the Universities
is conducted on what are regarded as business-
like methods. In most cases responsibility and
power are centred in one man,—the president,
—and, rightly or wrongly, he is thought to

exercise the most powerful influence on the destinies of his college—in striking contrast to the common view as to the average master of a college at Oxford or Cambridge. The president's is very far from being merely a position of dignified ease. He is expected to throw himself with true American energy into the task of advancing the interests of his college.

"4. There is very little tendency to rest satisfied with laurels already won, or to trade largely on the achievements of the past. Those of us who have spent the early years of our manhood at Cambridge or Oxford will always readily acknowledge their unequalled charm and greatness; but, if we really know anything of the spirit that animates the best American colleges, we will agree with your correspondent that 'it will be well for us if we prove as quick to see, as frank to admit, and as resolute to amend defects as they.'

*   *   *   *

"(St. John's Coll., Cambridge, and Columbia University, New York)."

APPENDIX II.

THE following extract from an article, which appeared in the *Boston Herald*, illustrates the statement of the first chapter of this book: "I shall be more restrained than Americans themselves in my criticisms" : —

"THE NATIONAL FAILING.

"Wendell Phillips, who had the great civic virtue of courage and of saying what he thought, once pointed out that entire equality and freedom in government and social structure 'almost invariably tend to make the individual subside into the mass and lose identity in the general whole.' In which case public opinion becomes not only omnipotent, but also omnipresent, and the result is 'that, instead of being a mass of individuals, each one fearlessly blurting out his own convictions,' the nation becomes, as he said the United States then was, compared with other nations, 'a mass of cowards.' 'More than all other peoples,' he added, 'we are afraid of each other.'

"It was this same combination of 'extraordinary mutual respect and kindness' and 'deficiency of moral independence' that Harriet Martineau noted when in this country in 1837. De Tocqueville also saw it, and Charles Follen commented upon it in contrast with the spirit of the Germany he had fled from to find greater liberty. Emerson and Channing, in their day, admitted the charge as justly resting against their countrymen. Now it occurs again in the letters of 'An Occasional Observer,' which are appearing in the London *Times* and which are based on a year's study of us by a man of much insight, whose observation has been international in scope, and which includes Russia and Asia as well as Europe.

.   .   .   .   .   .

.   .   .   .   .   .

" There are vital issues dividing men and parties in this country to-day, dividing also men within parties. How are they met? By square debate, plain speech, triumph of argument over argument, fact over fact, and then acquiescence of the minority in the decision of the majority because based on a victory in rational conflict? Not at all. Within parties and between parties the policy is to adjust, reduce friction to a minimum, bring about results through manipulation; and the electors will go to the polls next fall with nebulous notions as to principles, and vague sentiment controlling their choice as to men.

" The fault with President Roosevelt as a denouncer of men and of measures has been, not that he was candid, but that later, as a politician, he has made terms with the men he has denounced; and that he has resented equally candid talk in rebuttal from men and from corporations whom he has judged. It has been educational for the country to have an executive who was plain spoken, but it would have been vastly more so if there had been within his own party or in the party of opposition more men who had dared to question his judgments and oppose his will when, like all men of his temperament, he has erred or been unwise. And this has been the more necessary because of the swift mass movement or lurch of the American democracy in the direction of hero worship, and the tyranny of the public opinion of the hour."

APPENDIX III.

RECENTLY, individual workers, Jews and Christians, have cautiously introduced religious studies, if not religious services, into the University Settlement at New York; and Dr. Hamilton, its Warden, as all must recognise who have had the advantage of coming under his influence, is a profoundly religious man who, by the simplicity, integrity and devotion of his life, which has known the veiled prosperities of affliction, worthily represents Christianity to the multitudes of Jews in his institution and the still larger multitudes in its neighbourhood. At Hull House, Chicago, at least one modest Bible-class has been maintained for some years. At some Women's Settlements, such as Denison House, Boston, regular religious offices are observed by, and for, *the Residents*. At the Frances Willard Settlement, Boston, there are Christian services for the neighbourhood; and by many Institutional churches, in which some of the features of Social Settlements are found, continuous and aggressive religious work is done.

INDEX

Printed by MORRISON & GIBB LIMITED, *Edinburgh*

CPSIA information can be obtained
at www.ICGtesting.com
Printed in the USA
BVHW091030100822
644268BV00001B/22

9 780469 790735